D1165743

SUICIDE
AMONG
GIFTED CHILDREN
AND ADOLESCENTS

UNDERSTANDING
THE SUICIDAL MIND

SUICIDE
AMONG
GIFTED CHILDREN
AND ADOLESCENTS

UNDERSTANDING
THE SUICIDAL MIND

TRACY L. CROSS, PH.D., &
JENNIFER RIEDL CROSS, PH.D.

PRUFROCK PRESS INC.
WACO, TEXAS

Acknowledgements

Several people helped in creating this book. We would like to thank Lindsay Adams for her work, especially on updating the resources, and Natalie Dudnytska for her assistance with the chapter summaries. Thank you also to Lacy Compton for her work editing this book. We also thank Joel McIntosh for supporting this project, knowing that it would likely appeal to a relatively small readership.

Dedication

This book is dedicated to Ben and his family—
Roger, Sherry, and Amanda.

Edited by Lacy Compton

Cover and layout design by Allegra Denbo

ISBN-13: 978-1-61821-677-9

Prufrock Press Inc.
P.O. Box 8813
Waco, TX 76714-8813
Phone: (800) 998-2208
Fax: (800) 240-0333
http://www.prufrock.com

Table of Contents

FOREWORD TO THE FIRST EDITION[1]

I am pleased to provide a few words regarding Tracy Cross's unique contribution, *Suicide Among Gifted Children and Adolescents*. This book provides necessary information regarding the prevalence of the act itself, the risk factors associated with it, and helpful ideas on how schools can attempt to modify or eliminate this scourge.

Dr. Cross points out that "Clearly suicide is commonplace, pervasive in our society, and preventable." Because there is a multitude of evidence presented in this volume to verify that statement, we might reflect on why it is so rarely a topic considered in our schools and journals. The myth that "suicide is a sudden event that occurs out of nowhere and is unpredictable" maintains itself despite its falsity. Can it be that such a belief relieves all of us of responsibility to take action on this devastating problem? We are fortunate that Dr. Cross has collected this impressive data that calls on all of us to pay attention and act.

One of the useful discoveries from the data is the age most at risk. Adolescence appears to be the most vulnerable age, much more so than later college-age students. Apparently, many adolescents have not been able to develop positive coping skills to deal with the depression and social problems often attendant to that age and conclude from their hopelessness that ending things is the only answer.

The greater prevalence of suicide in states with higher rates of gun ownership is an interesting fact. Apparently, access to a

---

[1]   Dr. James J. Gallagher passed away on January 17, 2014. Because he was such a staunch supporter of our research, with permission, we have included Dr. Gallagher's foreword from the first edition of the book.

reliable tool may be the final factor in the recipe, because guns are much more reliable than poisons or knives to the person who has decided to act upon his or her despair.

The fact that suicide is no more prevalent among students with gifts and talents than among students with average abilities should not be seen as reassuring. In practically all other dimensions, being "gifted" is associated with positive factors such as greater health, friendships, etc. When such children prove just as vulnerable, that is proof again that it is personal ideation rather than reality that we are dealing with. Such children are as prone to depression and social isolation as other students.

In addition to the inevitable depression and despair among family and friends, we have a sense of loss of their special gifts: the sonata never written, the scientific cure never discovered, the political accomplishments never realized, the brilliant poetry never created. We can ill afford such loss of potential talent.

Cross's recommendation for schools are well advised. Both formal and informal screening of students should take place to identify early students at risk and to take positive action. Substitute behaviors can be encouraged, and positive behavior supports can be applied. A mental health committee to develop positive plans for individuals may operate similar to the Individualized Education Programs (IEPs) already in force and could be very helpful.

Also, the final section on national and state resources provides a good reference base for those looking for often-hard-to-find sources of information on this topic.

Dr. Cross has done his field, and all those who work in it, a valuable service in producing this volume. I believe it will be a much-quoted source for many years.

James J. Gallagher
University of North Carolina

PREFACE

TRACY L. CROSS

Although I have been somewhat aware of suicide since childhood, I have not been preoccupied with it or even particularly focused on it. I suspect that my longstanding interest in music and art have kept me close to people in two arenas wherein suicidal behavior has higher prevalence rates than average (Ludwig, 1995). I have also had numerous friends and acquaintances from the LGBTQ community, another group at higher than average risk for suicidal behavior. The single thread across my life is that I grew up surrounded by gifted and talented people. As I matured, I worried about some of my friends and acquaintances, as, occasionally, one would engage in suicidal ideation or make a suicide attempt. These experiences set the stage for my midcareer focus on the suicidal behavior of students with gifts and talents.

In April of 1994, while I was watching MTV News, I learned of the suicide of the alternative band Nirvana's singer-songwriter Kurt Cobain. I realized that we had lost an important musician and leader of disenfranchised youth. I feared that there would likely be a pronounced effect on the Cobain followers. For several months prior to Cobain's death, I had been involved in a yearlong evaluation of a residential high school for intellectually gifted students (Academy). Within a couple of weeks of Cobain's death, I was contacted by the dean of the college of education that administered the Academy and was apprised that it was prom night and there had been a suicide within the school's student body. I also learned that the suicide had occurred one block away from the Academy's campus. I met the dean at the Academy to help, prior to his informing the students what had happened. The dean had the very difficult responsibility of telling the students, during their prom, about the suicide of one of their popular student leaders.

I learned that same evening that a former student of the same school had killed himself a few months before while in a mental health institution. This student had been sent home from the school following a brief period of attendance, after a series of inappropriate behaviors were documented. The student spent a month in a mental health facility, came home for one day, was returned to the mental health facility, and later hanged himself in the facility. The school learned after his death that he had a long history of mental health problems and had made several attempts to kill himself before he attended the Academy. None of this information was shared with the Academy until after his death.

A task force was created by the dean to: (a) conduct a postvention, (b) prevent another suicide, and, (c) study the suicides at the school. A postvention is a plan to enter an environment after a tragedy or crisis and help ease the pain of those in the environment. Services were provided to students, families, and some faculty and staff after determining the extent to which individual community members were at risk. Postventions also attempt to prevent suicide contagion from occurring. To those ends, all students who were designated as at risk were attended to personally and over time. During the following summer months, a third student associated with the school killed himself at his original home high school. His suicidal journal entry is included at the beginning of the first chapter of this book. He was the third student who had attended the Academy for some period of time who had died by his own hand. In the ensuing 23 years, no additional suicides have occurred among students attending the Academy.

These three suicides required intensive, long-term study to understand. Three psychological autopsies were conducted, culminating in a special issue of the *Journal of Secondary Gifted Education* in 1996. Considerable study of the school environment was also undertaken before, during, and after the postvention. Eighteen months after the third suicide occurred, the dean asked me to take over the Academy as its Executive Director. Several policies had been changed as a function of the task force recommendations, including hiring a full-time clinical psychologist to work in the school. I was asked to stay as Executive Director of the school for a semester to try to calm the employees of the school, as the university's board of trustees was scheduled to vote on whether to shut the school down. Their concerns included both the suicides and a high level of acrimony that existed between the faculty and the Academy's administration. I ended up staying at the Academy for approximately 9 years, with my primary objective being the students' mental well-being.

CONFLUENCE OF EVENTS

I was trained as an educational psychologist and a school psychologist with a background in counseling, a passion in neuropsychology, and a focus on adolescents and gifted students. Over time, my specialty became the psychology of students with gifts and talents. Most of my research over the past 33 years has been focused in this area. Topics such as social coping, lived experience, and stigma of giftedness established the foundation for my shift to studying suicidal behavior. During this 30+ year period, I have run programs and a residential high school for gifted students and founded the Center for Gifted Studies and Talent Development and the Institute for Research on the Psychology of Gifted Students at Ball State University (BSU). Currently, I serve as Executive Director of the Center for Gifted Education at William & Mary, where I hold an endowed chair entitled The Jody and Layton Smith Professor of Psychology and Gifted Education. For 10 years prior to my stint at William & Mary, I served BSU as the George and Frances Ball Distinguished Professor of Psychology and Gifted Studies. I recently created the Institute for Research on the Suicide of Gifted Students at William & Mary.

Since beginning the psychological autopsies in 1994, I have focused much of my research on the suicidal behavior of students who are gifted and talented. I have written numerous articles and book chapters and made a multitude of presentations, all leading up to this book. This book is intended to provide an easy-to-read compilation of research that applies to the suicidal behavior of school-aged children and adolescents. More specifically, the book emphasizes the school as the context for observing students with gifts and talents. School is the single location that brings together teachers, counselors, administrators, and parents with the potential for monitoring and preventing suicide. Schools provide windows into the lives of students in ways that do not exist otherwise. For example, students develop patterns of behavior that foretell problems. Friendships, frustrations, relationships, alcohol and/or drug use, and academic achievement can all be monitored and interventions can be put in place before these lead to the death of a student.

An important second reason for placing the school at the center of this work is because it allows for four groups of adults (teachers, counselors, administrators, and parents), and others as need be, to collaborate for the best interest of the child. Parents have a good sense of their children, and often overhear things said by their children's friends. Teachers see changes in achievement and friendships and examples of bullying. Counselors often get brought in when there is a problem (although for some gifted students, teachers and counselors become their friends). Counselors also have training about social and emotional development that is quite valuable, plus many of the predictable issues of students with gifts and talents are related to topics about which the counselors are knowledgeable. Administrators tend to see a big picture that includes patterns, tendencies, and structures that are salient to the topic of creating a healthy school environment. Combined, this group makes for a powerful and informed force working to prevent suicide among students with gifts and talents. It is my hope that this book might help us prevent suicide among this population and any other children with whom we have contact.

PREFACE

JENNIFER RIEDL CROSS

My history with suicide has been tangential to Tracy's. I have been an onlooker as he became immersed in this difficult topic to which he was drawn in as a researcher and remained involved out of compassion. As a mother, I am concerned about the well-being of any child who considers ending his or her own life. In 1978, the philosopher Michel Foucault wrote of the "Right of death and power of life" (p. 134), in which he described suicide as a form of empowerment. It is an expression of power over another to take away a person's ability to do what he or she wants to do to relieve his or her suffering. Tracy and I come at this from a different place. Although biology is involved in some suicidal behavior, we believe conditions can play a powerful role in fostering a mindset that leads to suicide. Rather than disempowering individuals who want to take their own lives, we want to empower them by identifying the conditions that have led them to this place and showing them the way out. It is the conditions that we want to understand, so that we can propose ways of improving them for anyone—young or old—who feels hopeless enough to think that suicide is the only escape from pain. Exceptional individuals face unique challenges and students with gifts and talents are, by definition, exceptional. Our purpose here is to use what we know about students with gifts and talents to turn around what might appear to them to be hopeless situations.

CHAPTER 1

INTRODUCTION

I am having trouble deciding were [sic] to kill myself. I can either do it here [home]
when no one is home
call the police before so they can clean up so my family won't have to discover me
There is a chance the police would get there too soon and save me
My family would probably have very bad memories if they knew I did it in one of our trees
I can do it somewhere else someone would find me, call the police, my family would never see me
This would receive more publicity, which would be shitty for my parents and friends
Even though both are flawed I believe doing it somewhere else is the best option.

The preceding statements were the last journal entry of an intellectually gifted adolescent who completed suicide. It is presented as it was found relative to spacing, spelling, and overall appearance. A few days after writing the entry, the 16-year-old hanged himself in the rafters of the bus stop in front of his local high school. This was the first piece of information that Tracy obtained upon taking on the psychological autopsy of this gifted student.

The death of a child is a parent's worst nightmare. It represents many of the fears and doubts that raising children today elicit. Many people in society believe that being gifted makes one more vulnerable to suicide. Others believe the opposite—that giftedness provides protection from suicidal behavior. In either case, when a child dies by his or her own hand, nothing creates greater suffering and sense of loss, and nothing is a greater tragedy for society. This book explores the phenomenon of suicide among students with gifts and talents. It attempts to provide the reader a coherent picture of what suicidal behavior is and will clarify what is known and what is unknown about the phenomenon. The book will introduce two major theories of suicide with compelling explanatory power. Information that illustrates the lived experience of gifted students is provided that sets the stage for an emerging model of the suicidal behavior of this population. This model sheds light on the suicidal mind of students with gifts and talents. Based on recommendations derived from traditional suicide research and the research specific to those who are gifted, we provide information on what can be done to prevent suicides among these students. The book ends with considerable resources available to help.

To that end, the book is divided into relatively brief chapters that are based on empirical research, direct observation, literature review, other researchers' findings and arguments, and a model emerging from years of study. The book represents the level of understanding possible at this time in history. The primary motivation to write this book is to help keep our students alive. With that in mind, information about suicide, description of the lives of students with gifts and talents, and information about preventing suicide are provided.

In addition to raising the consciousness of adults interested in this topic, we will offer a carefully drafted narrative that stays as close to the research base as possible. From this, we hope to raise awareness of the suicidal behavior of students with gifts and talents, spurring additional efforts to be put in place to prevent suicides. We also hope that additional research will be conducted on the topic.

WHAT IS SUICIDE?

To begin, it makes sense to define suicide. Suicide is often defined as a successful act to end one's own life. It is an intentional act. As simple and direct as it sounds, it has engendered considerable study during the 20th and 21st centuries. Suicide has been acknowledged and written about for thousands of years and its meanings vary greatly based on the cultural context in which it occurs. Durkheim (1951) claimed that "There are two sorts of extra-social causes to which one may, *a priori*, attribute an influence on the suicide rate: they are organic-psychic dispositions and the nature of the physical environment" (p. 57). From committing *hara kiri* as an act of taking responsibility for failure, embarrassment, or shame, to dying to avoid responsibility, to dying as a culmination of myriad psychological factors, the context and historical zeitgeist in which suicide occurs matters. This book concentrates on ending one's life in Western society, particularly in the United States. It emphasizes the phenomenon in the second half of the 20th and the beginning of the 21st centuries.

SUICIDAL BEHAVIOR

If I throw myself off Lookout Mountain
No more pain my soul to bare
No more worries about paying taxes
What to eat, what to wear
Who will end up with my records?
Who will end up with my tapes?
Who will pay my credit card bills?
Who's gonna pay for my mistakes?
    —*"Lookout Mountain" by the Drive-By Truckers*

A more comprehensive conception of suicide is actually called *suicidal behavior* and includes three behaviors: ideation, attempts, and completions. The song lyrics above reveal the subject's thoughts about suicide, an example of suicide ideation. Considerable study has focused on suicide ideation, as it is widely believed by suicidologists to exist in virtually all completed suicides.

Suicide attempts are just that, efforts to die that fail. Completed suicides are defined as killing oneself intentionally. In this book, we use the term *completed* in lieu of *committed* when describing suicide. This linguistic change is important, as it reflects the fact that suicides are associated with mental health issues, not legal matters, as it has been considered to be for many years. Moreover, those who work with families of people who have taken their own lives stress the importance of destigmatizing suicide and the descriptor "completed" is both more appropriate and helpful in reducing stigmatization (B. Ball, personal communication, 1992). Another phrase that avoids the appearance of criminalization is "death by suicide."

Until recently, there was a fourth category of suicidal behavior called *gestures*. These were originally defined as unsuccessful suicide attempts that were not intended to actually result in death, but some considered any type of failed attempt a gesture (Heilbron, Compton, Daniel, & Goldston, 2010). Such a classification of suicidal behavior proved to be problematic when clinicians or others who might be able to help attempted to interpret "intent"—sometimes concluding the suicidal behavior was simply a cry for help or an effort to manipulate, and therefore, not genuine and less urgent (Heilbron et al., 2010). Eliminating the term from the recommended nomenclature reduces the possibility that any suicidal behavior will be dismissed (e.g., Crosby, Ortega, & Melanson, 2011). Terms such as *nonsuicidal self-harm* or *nonsuicidal self-directed violence* are now recommended (Crosby et al., 2011; Heilbron et al., 2010).

Figure 1 illustrates the relationship among the three suicidal behaviors. One of the important ideas being conveyed by this simple figure is that virtually all suicides occur after a person has engaged in suicide ideation. It becomes the background that sets the stage for attempts and completions. Secondly, many more people think about suicide than attempt or complete combined.

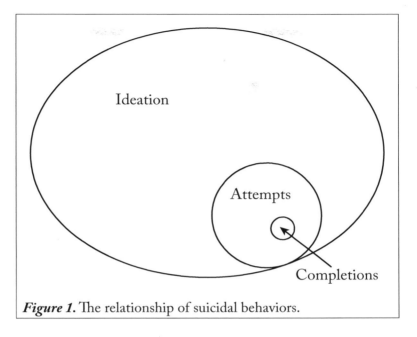

Figure 1. The relationship of suicidal behaviors.

Finally, there are many times more numbers of attempts compared to numbers of completions. This completion ratio plays out somewhat differently based upon ethnicity and gender and access to lethal means to harm oneself. This book focuses on suicidal behavior among students with gifts and talents. To get to that, however, basic information about suicide in general must set the stage.

KEY POINTS

❖ This book will discuss the phenomenon of suicide in the modern Western society, two major theories of suicide, a new model applied to students with gifts and talents, recommendations for suicide prevention, and available resources.

❖ Suicide is an intentional act of ending one's own life.

❖ The relationship of suicidal behaviors—ideation, attempts, and completions—was discussed.

- Ideation—thinking about suicide
- Attempts—efforts to die that fail
- Completions—killing oneself intentionally

CHAPTER 2

A BRIEF HISTORY OF COMPLETED SUICIDES

To understand suicidal behavior, specialists study prevalence rates. To that end, suicidologists rely on an equation: the number of people who complete suicide per 100,000 people per age group (X # per 100,000). For example, Table 1 reveals that for all age groups in 2014 there was an average prevalence rate of 13.0 per 100,000 people. Given that rates are established in age bands (i.e., 5–14, 15–24, 25–34, 35–44, 45–54, 55–64, 65–74, 75–84, 85+), analyzing the particular prevalence rate by age can be considered historically and comparatively. We can consider the range in prevalence rates over time and as compared to the other age bands. We can consider historic effects and emerging patterns. All of these comparisons can be made, but only for completed suicides, far less so for ideation and attempts.

Comparisons can also be made geographically (see Tables 2 and 3). The analysis of suicide rate by census region shows that the prevalence rate of all age groups combined in the Northeast (12.2 per 100,000) is well below the national average, while the prevalence rate in the West (18.7 per 100,000) is considerably higher. Of the 10 states with the highest prevalence rates, eight are Western states, with the highest rates occurring in Montana, Alaska, New Mexico, Wyoming, and Utah. The fewest absolute total numbers of suicides occurred in Rhode Island (113), while California had the greatest number (4,214).

In considering these varied rates by state, we speculated that states with the highest percentage of gun ownership might

Table 1
Rates of Suicide in the United States per 100,000 People

Year	Ages 5–14	Ages 15–24	Ages 25–34	Ages 35–44	Ages 45–54	Ages 55–64	Ages 65–74	Ages 75–84	Ages 85+	All ages*
2014	1.0	11.6	15.1	16.6	20.2	18.8	15.6	17.5	19.3	13.0
2013	1.0	11.1	14.8	16.2	19.7	18.1	15.0	17.1	18.6	12.6
2012	0.8	11.1	14.7	16.7	20.0	18.0	14.0	16.8	17.8	12.6
2011	0.7	11.0	14.6	16.2	19.8	17.1	14.1	16.5	16.9	12.3
2010	0.7	10.5	14.0	16.0	19.6	17.5	13.7	15.7	17.6	12.1
2009	0.6	10.0	13.1	16.1	19.2	16.4	13.7	15.8	16.4	11.8
2008	0.5	9.9	13.2	15.9	18.6	16.0	13.6	16.1	16.4	11.6
2007	0.5	9.6	13.3	15.7	17.7	15.3	12.4	16.2	17.0	11.3
2006	0.5	9.8	12.7	15.2	17.2	14.4	12.4	15.8	17.3	11.0
2005	0.7	9.9	12.7	15.1	16.5	13.7	12.4	16.8	18.3	10.9
2004	0.7	10.3	12.9	15.2	16.6	13.7	12.2	16.3	17.6	11.0
2003	0.6	9.6	12.9	15.0	15.9	13.7	12.6	16.4	17.9	10.8
2002	0.6	9.8	12.8	15.3	15.8	13.5	13.4	17.7	18.9	10.9
2001	0.7	9.9	12.8	14.7	15.1	13.2	13.2	17.4	17.8	10.7
2000	0.7	10.2	12.0	14.5	14.4	12.1	12.5	17.6	19.6	10.4
1999	0.6	10.1	12.7	14.3	13.9	12.2	13.4	18.1	19.3	10.5

*Age-adjusted rate

Note. Data retrieved from Kochanek, Murphy, Xu, and Tejada-Vera (2016).

Table 2
Suicide Rate by Region (2014)

Region	Rate per 100,000
Midwest	13.8
Northeast	12.2
South	13.6
West	18.7
Overall	13.0

Note. Data compiled from Kochanek et al. (2016) based on U.S. Census Bureau (n.d.) regions.

correspond with the highest rankings of completed suicide. The logic is that access to lethal means is an important correlate of suicide. In fact, this hypothesis has some support in the rates of gun ownership. A study of firearms ownership and social gun culture (Kalesan, Villarreal, Keyes, & Galea, 2016) can be used to give context to this argument. The states highest in suicide rate also have high rates of gun ownership—Montana (suicide prevalence rate 23.9; 52.3% gun ownership), Alaska (22.1; 61.7%), New Mexico (21; 49.9%), and Wyoming (20.6; 53.8%); while the states lowest in suicide rate also have low rates of gun ownership—New York (8.1; 10.3%), Maryland (8.2; 20.7%), Massachusetts (8.2; 22.6%), New Jersey (8.3; 11.3%), and Connecticut (9.8; 16.6%).

The following data are taken from a variety of CDC reports, including the National Vital Statistics Reports and the CDC WISQARS data reporting system (CDC, 2017b; Kochanek et al., 2016; see also http://www.cdc.gov/nchs/products/nvsr.htm). This information helps us to visualize and understand patterns of suicidal behavior in the U.S.

- ❖ 1.6% of all deaths are from suicide.
- ❖ On average, one suicide occurs every 11.9 minutes.
- ❖ Suicide is the 10th leading cause of death for all Americans.
- ❖ Suicide is the second leading cause of death for young people aged 15–24.

Table 3
Suicide Rate by State (2014)

Rank	State	Number	Rate per 100.00
1	Montana	251	23.9
2	Alaska	167	22.1
3	New Mexico	449	21.0
4	Wyoming	120	20.6
5	Utah	559	20.5
6	Idaho	320	20.0
7	Colorado	1,083	19.9
8	Nevada	573	19.6
9	Oklahoma	736	19.1
10	Vermont	124	18.7
11	Oregon	782	18.6
12	West Virginia	359	18.1
13	Arizona	1,244	18.0
14	New Hampshire	247	17.8
14	North Dakota	137	17.8
16	Arkansas	515	17.3
17	South Dakota	141	17.1
18	Missouri	1,017	16.3
19	Kentucky	728	16.0
20	Maine	220	15.7
20	Kansas	455	15.7
22	South Carolina	753	15.2
23	Washington	1,119	15.2
24	Tennessee	997	14.8
25	Indiana	948	14.3
25	Louisiana	679	14.3
27	Florida	3,035	13.9
28	Hawaii	204	13.8

Table 3, *continued*

Rank	State	Number	Rate per 100.00
29	Nebraska	251	13.4
30	Pennsylvania	1,817	13.3
30	Michigan	1,354	13.3
32	Delaware	126	13.2
33	North Carolina	1,352	13.1
33	Wisconsin	769	13.1
35	Alabama	715	13.0
36	Iowa	407	12.9
36	Virginia	1,123	12.9
38	Georgia	1,295	12.6
38	Ohio	1,491	12.6
40	Mississippi	380	12.5
41	Minnesota	686	12.2
41	Texas	3,254	12.2
43	California	4,214	10.5
43	Illinois	1,398	10.5
45	Rhode Island	113	10.1
46	Connecticut	379	9.8
47	New Jersey	786	8.3
48	Massachusetts	596	8.2
49	Maryland	606	8.2
50	New York	1,700	8.1
51	District of Columbia	52	7.8
	Overall	42,826	13.0

Note. Data retrieved from Kochanek et al. (2016).

- ❖ Suicide is the fourth leading cause of death for 25–44 year olds.
- ❖ Suicide is the second leading cause of death among college students (Turner, Leno & Keller, 2013).
- ❖ Male suicides occur at nearly 3 times the rate of female suicides. In 2015, 33,994 males died by suicide, while 10,199 females died by suicide.
- ❖ In the U.S., death by suicide occurs more than twice as frequently as death by homicide. In 2015, 44,193 completed suicide, while 17,793 were victims of homicide.
- ❖ An estimated 1.3 million Americans age 18 and over attempted suicide in 2014 (CDC, 2015a).

Clearly suicide is commonplace, pervasive in our society, and preventable. Suicidologists are becoming increasingly more sophisticated about the phenomenon. However, preventing suicidal behavior is complicated and requires the expertise of myriad professionals. For example, policy makers, healthcare professionals, researchers, philosophers, educators, and others have great potential for helping fix this societal problem.

An examination of suicide rates over an extended time period allows trends to be studied (see Table 4 and Figure 2). Across time, the youngest group has had the lowest incidence rates, while the highest rates were in the oldest groups. The data show that adolescents were less likely to complete suicide than adults. However, the trends over time for these groups were very different. Since 1950, the overall suicide rate has increased from 11.4 to 13.6. During this time span, youth (ages 5–24) suicide rates have more than doubled, while older adult (ages 55–85+) suicide rates have declined dramatically. The suicide rates for the 35–54 age group have remained relatively constant. In 1950, the suicide rates for older adults (26.8 to 31.1) were more than 5 times the rate for adolescents aged 15 to 24 (4.5). By 2015, the rates for older adults ranged from 15.3 to 19.4 while the rate for adolescents was 12.5. In 2015, the rate for older adults was less than twice the rate for adolescents. Thus, although the current rates for youth suicide may

Table 4
A 60-Year Look at Prevalence Rates

Year	All Ages	Ages 5–14	Ages 15–24	Ages 25–34	Ages 35–44	Ages 45–54	Ages 55–64	Ages 65–74	Ages 75–84	Ages 85+
1950	11.4	0.2	4.5	9.1	14.3	20.9	26.8	29.6	31.1	28.8
1960	10.6	0.3	5.2	10	14.2	20.7	23.7	23	27.9	26
1970	11.6	0.3	8.8	14.1	16.9	20	21.4	20.8	21.2	19
1980	11.9	0.4	12.3	16	15.4	15.9	15.9	16.9	19.1	19.2
1990	12.4	0.8	13.2	15.2	15.3	14.8	16	17.9	24.9	22.2
2000	10.4	0.7	10.2	12	14.5	14.4	12.1	12.5	17.6	19.6
2010	12.4	0.7	10.5	14	16	19.6	17.5	13.7	15.7	17.6
2015	13.6	1.0	12.5	15.7	17.1	20.3	19.0	15.3	17.9	19.4

Note. Rates are per 100,000; Data compiled from Centers for Disease Control and Prevention (2009, 2017a); Non-age-adjusted data.

13

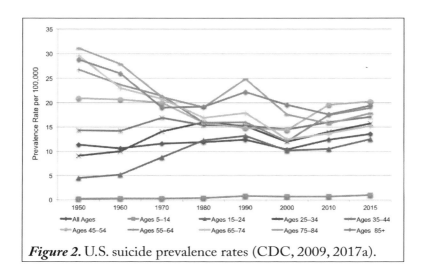

Figure 2. U.S. suicide prevalence rates (CDC, 2009, 2017a).

not appear to be disproportionate to the overall population rates, the trends observed over time for these groups are quite different.

TRENDS IN SUICIDAL BEHAVIOR

People have found myriad ways to kill themselves. Some of the popular methods from times past included poison, jumping from cliffs, and knives or swords. Contemporary approaches are wide ranging, from firearms to hanging. In some cases, such as car wrecks or death in a police shooting, intentionality may be unclear. A suicidal person may have intentionally crashed his or her car or induced a police officer to shoot. In such situations, psychological autopsies are a useful tool to determine cause of death relative to intent. More on psychological autopsy will appear in Chapter 6.

Firearms, suffocation, and poisons (including drugs/pharmaceuticals) are the most common methods of suicide. In recent times, important differences have existed between males and females relative to suicide attempts, completions, and approaches taken. Tables 5 and 6 illustrate the differences.

Table 5
Suicide Methods Used in the U.S. (2015); N = 44,193

Method	Percent of Total Suicides	Number of Suicides
Firearms	49.8%	22,018
Hanging, strangulation, suffocation	26.8%	11,855
Poisons	15.4%	6,816
All other methods	8.0%	3,504

Note. Data compiled from CDC (2017a).

Table 6
Suicide Methods by Gender (2015)

Method	Men (n = 33,994)		Women (n = 10,199)	
	Percent of Total	Number of Suicides	Percent of Total	Number of Suicides
Firearms	55.6%	18,910	30.5%	3,108
Hanging, strangulation, suffocation	26.9%	9,134	26.7%	2,721
Poisons	10.0%	3,407	33.4%	3,409
All other methods	7.5%	2,543	9.4%	961

Note. Data compiled from CDC (2017a).

Table 7 illustrates suicide-related behavior among students in grades 9–12 during the 12 months prior to the survey being conducted in 2015. The grouping of students aged 15–24 into one category in National Vital Statistics Reports masks developmental differences among those who engage in suicidal behavior. The American College Health Association and the Centers for Disease Control Division of Adolescent and School Health each collect data that can be compared to see these developmental differences (see Table 8; American College Health Association, 2016; CDC,

Table 7
Suicide-Related Behaviors of Students in Grades
9–12 in the U.S. (2015); N = 15,624

Behavior (During the 12 Months Before the Survey)	Prevalence Rate (%)
Seriously considered attempting suicide	17.7
Made a plan about how they would attempt suicide	14.6
Attempted suicide one or more times	8.6
Suicide attempt resulting in an injury, poisoning, or an overdose that had to be treated by a doctor or nurse	2.8

Note. Data retrieved from *2015 Youth Risk Behavior Survey*, Tables 25 and 27 (CDC, 2016).

2016). The two reports survey similar numbers of high school and college students. For example, the CDC's 2015 Youth Risk Behavior Survey high school sample was 15,624 students from across the U.S., and the 2015 ACHA sample was 16,760 students from 40 colleges and universities across the U.S. The high school students represent a heterogeneous group while college students would be a more selective group relative to general ability, academic achievement, and life experience. The data from these two reports show significantly lower rates of (a) seriously considering and (b) attempting suicide for college students compared to high school students. In 2015, high school students attempted suicide at a rate that was 7 times greater than the rate for college students, and seriously considered suicide at a rate that was nearly 3 times higher than that for college students. From 2001 to 2009, both groups showed a positive downward trend in suicidal behavior, but there has been an uptick in recent years.

High school and college students will generally fall into the 15–24 age group, which had a dip in its steady increase in completed suicides in the first decade of the 21st century (see Table 4). This downward trend has reversed according to 2015 data. Suicide ideation and attempts among both college and high school students (Table 8) reflect this overall trend. The differences between the two groups imply that high school students are at significantly

Table 8
Trends in Suicide-Related Behaviors of High School and College Students in the U.S.

	2001	2003	2005	2007	2009	2011	2015
Percent of high school students who seriously considered suicide in past 12 months	19.0	16.9	16.9	14.5	13.8	15.8	17.7
Percent of high school students who attempted suicide in past 12 months	8.8	8.5	8.4	6.9	6.3	7.8	8.6
Percent of undergraduate college students who seriously considered suicide in past 12 months	10.5	10.3	10.2	9.8	3.8	4.4	6.5
Percent of undergraduate college students who attempted suicide in past 12 months	1.8	1.3	1.5	1.6	0.7	0.7	1.2

Note. Data compiled from CDC (2013, 2016), and American College Health Association (2016).

higher risk for suicidal behaviors, particularly for suicide attempts, than college students. It may be that students find greater acceptance in the college environment than in the high school environment because they are able to find a peer group that readily accepts them as they are. For students who are nonmodal (e.g., high-ability students), or who possess characteristics that make them feel very different from most of their peers, finding this acceptance in high school can be difficult.

Acceptance in a peer group is not necessarily an explanation for differences in the nature of suicidal ideation between adolescents or young adults and the elderly. We can infer from developmental differences and life differences between these age groups that the rationalizations these individuals use to justify suicidal behaviors are profoundly different. Youth suicidal behavior tends to be driven by the desire to escape relatively temporary emotional pains (Shneidman, 1993), while the need to be free of chronic physical pain is a common rationalization of suicidal behavior for the elderly. Young people have immature notions of permanence compared to older people, and this becomes an essential factor in the suicide decision. Older people have a better sense of temporality because of their life experiences. Furthermore, the emotional pains of youth will subside, while the physical pains of the elderly often worsen. Therefore, suicide ideation is a qualitatively different phenomenon among diverse age groups.

As this summary of the available data indicates, completed suicides are a reality of modern society. In 2015, 36,277 people under the age of 65 died by suicide. The CDC calculates the number of years of potential life if these thousands of people had lived just to the age of 65 (CDC, 2015b). These 869,164 years of potential productivity, creativity, and social interactions were lost forever when they died. Some unknown number of the tens of thousands of deaths by suicide each year is likely to be of individuals with gifts and talents. In the next chapter, we will examine the research that offers clues to how we may identify and support the unique population that is the focus of this book.

KEY POINTS

❖ Suicidologists study prevalence rates that are established in age bands to understand suicidal behavior and to consider them historically and comparatively.

❖ Analysis of suicide rates by census region: Highest suicide rates in 2014 were recorded in the Western U.S., and the lowest rates were recorded in the Northeast.

- ❖ Access to lethal means is an important correlate of suicide. Hence, the states with the highest percentage of gun ownership correspond with the highest rankings of completed suicide.
- ❖ Suicide is the second leading cause of death among college students.
- ❖ Suicide is commonplace, pervasive to our society, and preventable.
- ❖ Policy makers, health care professionals, researchers, philosophers, educators, and others have great potential for helping prevent suicide.
- ❖ Examination of suicide prevalence rates from 1950–2015 showed that the suicide rate has been increasing, but at a more rapid pace for youth (ages 5–24), whose rates have nearly tripled.
- ❖ The most common contemporary approaches to completing suicide are firearms, followed by hanging or suffocation.
- ❖ High school students are at significantly higher risk for suicidal behaviors than college students.
- ❖ Suicide ideation is a qualitatively different phenomenon among diverse age groups.

CHAPTER 3

EXPANDING THE EPIDEMIOLOGICAL LENS FROM PREVALENCE RATES TO CORRELATES

To understand the specific research on students with gifts and talents and suicide, we must first illustrate the current knowledge of suicide among the general population of children, adolescents, and young adults beyond mere prevalence rates. There has been considerable research focused on how to predict completed suicides. From this research, risk factors have been identified. Risk factors are established statistically by correlating different traits, qualities, and behaviors with completed or attempted suicides. Initial studies of risk factors were designed somewhat atheoretically, by analyzing relationships among any variables that could be found and correlated. Over time, the research was improved by including theories of suicide, which were to varying degrees empirically validated, complementing the epidemiological data. Two especially important theories will be discussed in Chapter 4. They represent two different, but powerful theories for making sense out of suicidal behavior. They are psychache (Shneidman, 1993) and the suicide trajectory model (Stillion & McDowell, 1996). Building on these theories, later in the book we will offer a theory for the suicidal mind and suicidal behavior among students with gifts and talents.

It is important to understand not only how many people of different categories are engaged in suicidal behavior, but also to know what is associated (statistically speaking, correlated) with suicide. These correlates are often presented as being risk factors, although, to be clear, correlation is not the same as causation. Quite a bit of research has been conducted to uncover correlates of suicidal behaviors. Rudd et al. (2006) attempted to more fully distinguish between the risk factors and warning signs of suicide. He concluded that risk factors tend to be stable characteristics such as age, suicide attempts, and comorbidity, while warning signs are more transitory states such as psychache and hopelessness. Warning signs will be discussed more fully in later chapters.

RISK FACTORS FOR ADOLESCENT SUICIDE

Gould, Greenberg, Velting, and Shaffer (2003) conducted a review of a decade's worth of research on adolescent suicide and described the following as significant risk factors:

1. Psychiatric disorders such as depression and anxiety (referred to as comorbidity, which is very strongly associated with attempts and completions)
2. Substance abuse (can vary in type, but alcohol and other popular depressants are the more common types)
3. Cognitive and personality factors (e.g., hopelessness, coping skills, neuroticism)
4. Aggressive-impulsive behavior
5. Sexual orientation (homosexual, bisexual)
6. Friend or family member of someone with suicidal behavior
7. Parental psychopathology (e.g., depression, substance abuse)
8. Stressful life circumstances (e.g., interpersonal loss, legal/disciplinary)
9. Glamorization of suicide through media coverage

10. Access to lethal methods (e.g., firearms)

Because most of these are self-explanatory, we will only comment on three of them, beginning with sexual orientation (homosexual, bisexual). The risk does not arise from being homosexual or bisexual, per se. Rather, it derives from a person's lived experience of having a nonnormative sexual orientation in a society that rejects that identity. LGBTQ (lesbian, gay, bisexual, transgender, queer/questioning) youth are at risk for violence because of negative attitudes that permeate the society. These attitudes are the impetus for mistreatment, sometimes even from members of one's own family (Ryan, Huebner, Diaz, & Sanchez, 2009). Bullying rates are higher among LGBTQ youth, as well (Birkett, Espelage, & Koenig, 2009). These youth become homeless at a higher rate than their heterosexual peers and have a higher rate of sexual abuse (Coker, Austin, & Schuster, 2010). The compounding effect of rejection results in a higher risk of suicidal behavior among the LGBTQ population, a consistent finding in research (e.g., Grossman & D'Augelli, 2007; Russell & Joyner, 2001). To date, little research has focused on differences in suicidal behaviors or risk factors for the different subgroups, lumping all those together under the LGBTQ umbrella. More sophisticated research in this area is needed to identify how risk factors may differ for each group.

There has been evidence since the 18th century for the risk of number 9 on the list, glamorization of suicide through media coverage. The publication of Goethe's popular book *The Sorrows of Young Werther* in 1774, about a young man who died by suicide in response to societal and romantic rejection, was followed by fears and some evidence of imitation suicides that led to a ban of the book in some European countries (Jack, 2014). Suicides that follow a media event, from the publication of a book to news reports of a celebrity suicide have been called the *Werther effect*. The contemporary television series *13 Reasons Why* has been similarly prohibited in some schools and even countries out of fear that young people will imitate the suicide of the main character (Knapp, 2017; Roy, 2017).

Some research has borne out an increase in imitative suicides after such prominent sharing (e.g., Gould & Shaffer, 1986; Niederkrotenthaler et al., 2012). In the month after news reports of Marilyn Monroe's death by suicide in 1962, there was a 12% increase in the number of suicides across the U.S. (Phillips, 1974). Following the suicide of musician Kurt Cobain, there was considerable attention in the media. For weeks, MTV and other news outlets aired programs about the life, death, and music of Kurt Cobain. This suicide was one of the major news events of 1994, and given the growing competition at the time among the increasing number of 24-hour news stations, the amount of coverage was quite substantial. Although there was not an increase in suicides in the Seattle area in the weeks immediately after his death, there was a significant increase in calls to crisis hotlines (Jobes, Berman, O'Carroll, Eastgard, & Knickmeyer, 1996). The authors attribute this relative success to great attention to responsible reporting, a community call for comforting one another, and a personalization of the suffering Cobain's death had caused. Media outlets are increasingly being made aware of helpful and harmful practices in the reporting of suicides (John et al., 2017). The World Health Organization (WHO, 2008) offered guidelines for responsible reporting, such as avoiding sensationalizing the suicide and not publishing pictures or descriptions of the methods used.

The third risk factor to be noted is number 10 on the list: access to lethal methods (firearms). Of all of the 10 risk factors, this one draws the most concern from those who believe that it might have an effect on gun ownership. The issue is not about second amendment rights to own a gun, rather it is the fact that when a suicidal person has immediate access to lethal means of death, chances of a successful suicide increase. As noted in Chapter 2, where there are more firearms, rates of suicide are higher. Firearms are extremely effective in a suicide attempt. Based on emergency room statistics in 2001, the case fatality ratio (fatal:nonfatal injury) of successful efforts at self-harm with firearms was 85:15, for suffocation or hanging 69:31, but for poisoning or overdose it was only 2:98, and for cutting or piercing only 1:99 (Miller, Azrael, & Barber, 2012).

Gould et al.'s (2003) research is important because it brings together many previously conducted studies. The 10 risk factors of suicide become an important tool to help us understand variables associated with suicidal behavior. Although not causal per se, in some cases the correlations are quite strong. For example, it is very common for people who engage in suicidal behavior to also be experiencing depression or anxiety. This fact provides guidance about how to intervene to prevent suicide. Unfortunately, however, other correlates such as sexual orientation or whether a family member has completed suicide cannot be changed. Keep in mind that correlation is not causation. Even with the inherent limitations of relying on correlates as risk factors, knowing what these are greatly benefits our understanding and potential to intervene in positive ways to help prevent completed suicides. Note that suicide prevention will be discussed in Chapter 8.

The American Association of Suicidology (n.d.) offered the information presented in Table 9 as an easy-to-remember consensus of warning signs of suicide. Although not exactly the same as the previous list of factors associated with suicide offered by Gould et al. (2003), the "IS PATH WARM" acronym identifies variables that overlap considerably. It also uses language that is less technical, making it easier to read and share with others. It is important to note that millions of people live long lives with one or more of the risk factors we have described. Moreover, trying to predict actual suicide attempts from knowledge of an individual's risk factors has not been very successful.

An excellent visual illustrating factors that both make people vulnerable to, and protected from, completed suicides is included in Table 10 (adapted from White, 2016), a quick guide for adults who want to familiarize themselves with predisposing, contributing, precipitating, and protective factors by key content as broken down into the categories of individual, family, peer, school, and community. Individuals may be predisposed to considering suicide due to their prior experience, family history, or events in

Table 9
Consensus Warning Signs of Suicide (American Association of Suicidology, n.d.)

A person at risk for suicidal behavior most often will exhibit warning signs such as:

Letter	Represents	Description
I	Ideation	Expressed or communicated ideation • Threatening to hurt or kill him- or herself, or talking of wanting to hurt or kill him- or herself • Looking for ways to kill him- or herself by seeking access to firearms, available pills, or other means • Talking or writing about death, dying, or suicide when these actions are out of the ordinary
S	Substance Abuse	Increased substance (alcohol or drug) use
P	Purposelessness	No reasons for living; no sense of purpose in life
A	Anxiety	Anxiety, agitation; unable to sleep or sleeping all of the time
T	Trapped	Feeling trapped—like there's no way out
H	Hopelessness	Hopelessness
W	Withdrawal	Withdrawing from friends, family, and society
A	Anger	Rage, uncontrolled anger, seeking revenge
R	Recklessness	Acting reckless or engaging in risky activities, seemingly without thinking
M	Mood Changes	Dramatic mood changes

Table 10
Risk and Protective Factors Among Students With Gifts and Talents

Key Content	Predisposing Factors	Contributing Factors	Precipitating Factors	Protective Factors
Individual	• Previous suicide attempt • Depression, substance abuse, anxiety, bipolar disorder, or other mental health problems • Hopelessness • Persistent and enduring suicidal thoughts • History of childhood neglect, sexual or physical abuse • *Lack of trust in others*	• Rigid cognitive style • Poor coping skills *(hiding and denial of abilities)* • Limited distress tolerance skills • Substance misuse • Impulsivity • Aggression • Hypersensitivity/anxiety • *Desire for authenticity* • *Hiding oneself for long periods of time* • *Learning to code-switch* • *Overexcitabilities* • *Introversion* • *Perfectionism (self-, socially prescribed esp.)*	• Loss • Personal failure • *Academic failure* • Victim of cruelty, humiliation, violence • Individual trauma • Health crisis • *Crisis with authority*	• Individual coping, self-soothing, and problem-solving skills • Willingness to seek help • Good physical and mental health • Experience/feelings of success • Strong cultural identity and spiritual health • Living in balance and harmony • *Advanced cognitive abilities* • *Social information management skills* • *Long-term academic success*

Table 10, *continued*

Key Content	Predisposing Factors	Contributing Factors	Precipitating Factors	Protective Factors
Individual, continued		• *Persistent academic stress/ pressure* • *Long-term academic success*		
Family	• Family history of suicidal behavior/ suicide • Family history of mental disorder • Early childhood loss/separation or deprivation • *Family history of perfectionism*	• Family discord • Punitive parenting • Impaired parent-child relationships • Invalidating interpersonal environment • Multigenerational trauma and losses • *Mixed messages*	• Loss of significant family member • Death of family members, especially by suicide • Recent conflict	• Family cohesions and warmth • Positive parent-child connection • Positive role models • Active parental supervision • High and realistic expectations • Support and involvement of extended family and elders • Connection to ancestors

Table 10, *continued*

Key Content	Predisposing Factors	Contributing Factors	Precipitating Factors	Protective Factors
Peers	• Social isolation and alienation • *Lack of understanding* • *No intellectual peers* • *Anti-intellectualism*	• Negative attitudes toward help seeking • Limited/conflicted peer relationships • Suicidal behaviors among peers	• Interpersonal loss or conflict • Peer victimization • Rejection • Peer death by suicide	• Social competence • Healthy peer modeling • Peer friendship, acceptance, and support
School	• History of negative school experience • Lack of meaningful connection to school • *Anti-intellectualism*	• Reluctance/uncertainty about how to help among school staff • *Mixed messages*	• Failure • Expulsion • Disciplinary crisis • School-based harassment • *Misunderstood by school personnel*	• Success at school • Interpersonal connectedness/belonging • Supportive school climate • School engagement • Anti-harassment policies and practices • *Appropriate academic challenge* • *Opportunity to be with intellectual peers*

Table 10, *continued*

Key Content	Predisposing Factors	Contributing Factors	Precipitating Factors	Protective Factors
Community	• Multiple suicides • Community marginalization • Socioeconomic deprivation • *Anti-intellectualism*	• Sensational media portrayal of suicide • Access to firearms or other lethal methods • Uncertainty about how to help among key gatekeepers • Inaccessible community resources	• High profile/ celebrity death, especially by suicide • Conflict with law/ incarceration	• Opportunities for youth participation • Availability of resources • Community ownership • Control over services • Culturally safe healing practices • Opportunities to connect to land and nature
Sociopolitical	• Colonialism • Historical trauma • Cultural stress • Interlocking oppressions	• Racism • Sexism • Classism • Ableism • Heterosexism • *Anti-intellectualism*	• Social exclusion • Social injustice	• Social capital • Social justice • Social safety net • Social determinants of health

Note. Italicized items apply specifically to students with gifts and talents. Adapted with permission from *Preventing Youth Suicide: A Guide for Practitioners,* by J. White, 2016, Victoria, British Columbia: Ministry of Children and Family Development. Retrieved from http://www2.gov.bc.ca/assets/gov/health/managing-your-health/mental-health-substance-use/child-teen-mental-health/preventing_youth_suicide_practitioners_guide.pdf their community. The influence of these predispositions may be multiplied by contributing factors at every level. Events or circumstances can become precipitating factors that make suicidal thinking more likely. These factors can be tempered by protective factors such as those listed. We have added items to White's original table that are specific to students with gifts and talents. Table 10 provides the reader with information about ways that people are naturally protected from engaging in suicidal behavior and some ways to provide these protections. The big picture represents an optimistic and somewhat thorough overview of factors associated with suicidal behavior.

One can easily imagine a person grappling with some of the factors while benefitting from others. However, the degree of influence across the factors varies widely and some have not been empirically validated in a list like Gould et al.'s (2003) have been. However, once again, there is considerable overlap with other, more scientific lists. The gestalt of Table 10 is that it is more phenomenological than merely listing factors. Many of the terms and phrases in Table 10, such as *humiliation*, are powerful examples of human experience that can be quite motivating when combined with other factors, such as feeling trapped or hopeless. In essence, a person can become increasingly weighted down as the number and/or severity of the suicidal factors impacts him or her. This description of a phenomenological model of suicidal behavior is the image that we are moving the reader toward—away from a conception that is more associative or based on a list of factors.

Table 10 includes risk and protective factors from several perspectives, including the community. This particular perspective is usually outside the emphasis of any book that is more school-focused. It is included in this book, however, because schools are often situated within communities. Communities are also where media portrayals of suicide events of myriad famous people, such as the musician Chris Cornell or actor/comedian Robin Williams occur. It also supports the earliest contention of this book—that to understand suicides, one must understand the context in which they occur.

KEY POINTS

❖ Suicide risk factors have been defined in order to predict completed suicides by correlating traits, qualities, and behaviors with completed or attempted suicides.

❖ Two theories important for understanding suicidal behaviors are psychache (Shneidman, 1993) and the suicide trajectory model (Stillion & McDowell, 1996).

❖ Significant risk factors for adolescent suicide, as defined by Gould et al. (2003), include psychiatric disorders, substance abuse, and cognitive and personality factors.

❖ Sexual orientation becomes a risk factor depending upon the lived experience of a person or his or her treatment in society.

❖ Another risk factor is glamorization of suicide through media coverage (e.g., celebrity suicide).

❖ The access to lethal methods (e.g., firearms) risk factor is important because it increases chances of a successful suicide.

❖ Knowledge of risk factors benefits our understanding and potential to intervene in positive ways to help prevent completed suicides.

❖ Table 9, featuring information offered by the American Association of Suicidology, is a comprehensive way to remember consensus of warning signs of suicide (IS PATH WARM?).

❖ The suicide risk and protective factors table (Table 10; White, 2016) provides a phenomenological model of suicidal behavior.

CHAPTER 4

SUICIDE TRAJECTORY MODEL AND PSYCHACHE

Among the various theories associated with suicide, we have come to prefer two: Stillion and McDowell's (1996) suicide trajectory model and Shneidman's (1993) psychache. These two models seem to provide considerable explanatory power about suicidal behavior.

SUICIDE TRAJECTORY MODEL

Stillion and McDowell (1996) developed a theory-based model of suicide called the suicide trajectory model (STM; see Table 11), which includes associated risk factors. The emphasis of the theory is to predict risk for suicidal behavior.

The STM groups correlates of suicide into four categories (biological, psychological, cognitive, and environmental) that provide considerable breadth. This makes conceptual understanding of the numerous predictors of suicide in a theoretical manner manageable. It provides a conception of suicide that offers professionals numerous handles upon which to grasp as they try to prevent deaths. Metaphorically, it provides a categorical system of potential weights that lead the suicidal person in the direction of suicide. The theory attempts to coherently tie together the categories of factors. Stillion and McDowell (1996) stated:

Table 11

Suicide Trajectory Model Categories and Associated Risk Factors

Category	Risk Factors
Biological	Gender (male)
	Race (Native American, White)
	Genetic bases (parental psychopathy)
	Sexual orientation (homosexual, bisexual)
	Serotonin dysfunction
Psychological	Low self-esteem
	Depressed mood
	Feelings of hopelessness/helplessness
	Aggressive-impulsive tendencies
	Poor coping strategies
	Existential questions
Cognitive	Poor social problem solving
	Inflexible thinking
	Negative self-talk
	Rigidity of thought
Environmental	Familial dysfunction (impaired parent-child relationships)
	Social isolation
	Stressful life circumstances (interpersonal loss)
	Presence of lethal methods
	Exposure to suicide completers (friends/family)

As we move through life, we encounter situations and events that add their weight to each risk factor category. When the combined weight of these risk factors reaches the point where coping skills are threatened with collapse, suicidal ideation is born. Once present, suicidal ideation seems to feed upon itself. It may be exhibited in warning signs and may be intensified by trigger events. In the final analysis, however, when the suicide attempt is made, it occurs because of the contributions of the four risk categories. (p. 21)

The limitation to the STM, however, is that it is largely made up of correlations or variables associated with suicidal behavior with limited influence from within the person. This is where Shneidman's (1993) work picked up, as he moved the conversation from descriptive epidemiology and prediction with some explanation to a theory that has been empirically validated focusing on the subjective experiences of the suicidal person. We believe this to be the most important contribution to research on the suicidal mind.

PSYCHACHE

I never thought I'd die alone
I laughed the loudest who'd have known?
I trace the cord back to the wall
No wonder it was never plugged in at all
I took my time, I hurried up
The choice was mine, I didn't think enough
I'm too depressed to go on
You'll be sorry when I'm gone
    —"Adam's Song" by Blink 182

Edwin Shneidman was a clinical psychologist and arguably the father of suicidology and thanatology (the study of death and the care of the dying) in the U.S., who died in 2009. He spent his career focused on suicide, authoring 20 books and numerous articles about suicide, including one wherein he focused on survivors of suicide—1998's *The Suicidal Mind.* This book provides considerable information about the lived experience of suicide attempters: one of the three died, the second lived for several months before dying of infections, and the third survived but was disfigured by the attempt. Shneidman began the American Association of Suicidology and the journal *Suicide and Life Threatening Behavior.* He also coined the term *psychological autopsy.*

Psychological autopsy, while often used to determine equivocal deaths, has become an invaluable approach to studying the life of a person who completed suicide. Tracy and his colleagues employed this approach in their early research (Cross, Cook, & Dixon, 1996) and again later (Cross, Gust-Brey, & Ball, 2002). From his many years in the field working with clients and from previous research, Shneidman's (1993) theory asserted that suicide attempts come from the desire on the part of the person to escape intolerable psychological pain. He called this pain *psychache*. This profound pain's etiology includes several potential pathways and factors. Ultimately, when the pain is unbearable, suicide becomes the path to escape it.

Shneidman (1993) believed that suicide has four elements: (a) heightened inimicality (hostility), (b) exacerbation of perturbation, (c) increased constriction of intellectual focus, and (d) cessation. Shneidman (1981) described inimicality as "qualities within the individual that are unfriendly towards the self" (p. 222). Perturbation "reflects how 'shook up', ill at ease, or mentally upset the person is" (p. 223). Constriction reflects the suicidal person's dichotomous thinking and unwillingness to consider the effects of suicide on others. Cessation occurs due to the belief that ending one's life will end the unbearable pain (psychache).

Over the years, Shneidman and others grew increasingly interested in the role that hopelessness plays in suicidal behavior. A few others picked up on this idea. For example, a study by DeLisle and Holden (2009) revealed that psychache and hopelessness both contribute variance to the prediction of suicide. This suggests that each can be valuable to understanding and preventing suicide.

Rudd et al. (2006) attempted to distinguish between the risk factors and warning signs of suicide. They claimed that risk factors tend to be stable characteristics, such as age, history of attempts, and psychiatric diagnosis. Risk factors are thought to be distally related to suicide. On the other hand, warning signs such as psychache and hopelessness are thought to be proximally associated with suicidal behavior and suggest potentially imminent risk. Distal risk factors are thought to be the initial causative factors in the original environment, while proximal causes are current causative factors (Rudd et al., 2006).

Combining prevalence rates, correlates, and risk factors with the STM, Shneidman's (1993) theory of psychache, and the very recent research on hopelessness paints an increasingly comprehensive picture of the nature of suicide among the general population of the U.S. Despite the increasingly sophisticated level of understanding, it has proven to be very difficult to accurately predict suicide attempts and completions.

The STM provides us the capacity to look for students in distress. Shneidman's concept of psychache, plus the recent research on hopelessness, provides us with an excellent basic roadmap for understanding some of the salient aspects of the lived experience of suicidal behavior. When all of the variables are taken together, strategies and techniques for preventing suicide in school can be put in place. This will be explored later in the book in Chapter 8. But first, we will describe research that pertains to students with gifts and talents.

KEY POINTS

* ❖ Stillion and McDowell's (1996) theory-based suicide trajectory model includes associated risk factors that are grouped into four categories (biological, psychological, cognitive, and environmental).

* ❖ Edwin Shneidman's (1993) work on suicide moves from descriptive epidemiology and prediction to a theory that has been empirically validated focusing on the subjective experiences of the suicidal person.

* ❖ The importance of Edwin Shneidman's input into suicidology and thanatology was discussed.

* ❖ Shneidman's (1993) theory asserts that suicide attempts come from the desire on the part of the person to escape intolerable psychological pain.

❖ Four elements of suicide as defined by Shneidman (1993) are: (a) heightened inimicality (hostility), (b) exacerbation of perturbation, (c) increased constriction of intellectual focus, and (d) cessation.

❖ Rudd et al. (2006) attempted to distinguish between the risk factors (distally related to suicide) and warning signs (proximally associated with suicidal behavior) of suicide.

❖ Understanding the nature of suicide will help us to develop and use strategies and techniques for preventing suicide in schools.

CHAPTER 5

RESEARCH ON THE SUICIDAL BEHAVIOR OF STUDENTS WITH GIFTS AND TALENTS

This topic is so important that it has drawn considerable attention from professionals who work on behalf of students with gifts and talents. A great deal has been published claiming that either gifted students are more susceptible to suicidal behavior or they have qualities that naturally protect them from this behavior. Although reasonable logic exists on both sides of the argument, neither side has brought any data to back up their assertions. Therefore, those articles will generally not be included in this book.

As noted in Chapter 2, typically the first step in studying suicide among subgroups begins with establishing the total numbers and prevalence rates. Perhaps surprisingly in the year 2017, the actual numbers and prevalence rates of suicide among students with gifts and talents are unknown. This is due in part because of the lack of a consensus definition of a gifted population (Cross, 1996a, 1996b; Delisle, 1986). Without knowing exactly who they are, we cannot be accurate in our estimates of prevalence rates. Even if there was greater consensus on a definition, the CDC (2015c) does not maintain detailed statistics of suicide deaths to indicate demographics such as giftedness.

Making this determination even more difficult is the fact that, due to our commitment to local control, school districts often have differing definitions of giftedness. Consequently, if a student with gifts and talents happens to die via suicide in a school district that does not use the same definition as his or her previous school, then that information has little chance of becoming known. Each of the examples noted above has nuances that make following giftedness as a demographic variable almost impossible. Even with profound impediments to knowing absolute numbers and prevalence rates, like their nongifted peers, it is quite likely that gifted students are completing suicide and the incidence of suicidal behavior among both groups has followed the basic pattern wherein rates have recently increased (Cross, 1996a, 1996b). Consequently, it is judicious to assume that the rates of suicidal behavior of gifted and nongifted same-aged students are quite similar unless empirically proven otherwise. Although we cannot know whether the incidence of suicide among students with gifts and talents is different from that of their peers in the general population, we can, however, describe the few studies that offer clues into this murky phenomenon.

Several large-scale studies have explored the relationship between IQ and suicidal behaviors, with mixed results. In some studies, researchers have found that, as IQ increases, so does suicidal ideation, although only by a small amount. Other researchers have found the opposite relationship, with low IQ associated with greater risk of suicidal behavior. When examining the relationship between achievement and suicidal ideation, we see similar conflicting findings, with some studies identifying high levels of achievement as an apparent risk factor and others finding it protective (see Cross & Cross, 2017b, for a review). In our review of this research, we have concluded that, in studies designed specifically to explore intelligence or achievement and suicidal ideation, the findings appear more positive for students with gifts and talents. When studies utilize existing data, sometimes from disparate sources, the findings suggest a suicide risk is associated with advanced intellect, but these findings should be interpreted with caution.

In the few studies comparing suicidal ideation between gifted and nongifted samples, there are not significant differences in ideation scores (Baker, 1995; Cassady & Cross, 2006; Cross, Cassady,

& Miller, 2006; Metha & McWhirter, 1997). In Tracy's studies with colleagues, rates of suicidal ideation in the gifted sample were similar to the norm group on Reynolds's (1987) Adult Suicide Ideation Questionnaire. Exploring the data further, however, they found that the factor structure of suicidal ideation was different in the gifted sample from the norm (Cassady & Cross, 2006). Whereas Reynolds found three factors in his norm sample of adolescents—(a) wishes and plans, (b) focus on responses and aspects of others, and (c) morbid ideation—they found four factors. The gifted student sample factors were (a) wishes and plans, (b) morbid fixation, (c) social isolation, and (d) social impact. A positive outcome of this study is the possibility that exists for tailoring interventions to work with this unique ideation pattern, focusing on adolescents with specific risk orientations. For example, students who strongly indicate they have wishes or plans for suicide should be observed closely and any potentially lethal objects (i.e., guns, knives, drugs) should be kept away from them. Interventions for those who indicate they are socially isolated can focus on developing social skills and improving self-esteem.

In most cases, gifted students have been identified for their advanced cognitive abilities. If suicide attempts begin with suicide ideation, and gifted persons have the ability or inclination to think about suicide in a different way from their nongifted peers, it is important to further explore their ideation. Typical intervention methods used for nongifted adolescents may be ineffective or inappropriate for suicidal students who are gifted (Cross, 2008). Stillion, McDowell, and May (1984) found that adolescent females who scored higher on IQ tests were less likely to agree with the reasons for suicide than those with lower IQ scores. This suggests a connection between cognitive abilities and the belief that suicide is a viable solution. Although how gifted individuals think about suicide requires further exploration, at this time we need to realize that students with gifts and talents engage in suicidal ideation differently than their nongifted peers, if not at different rates. This may have important ramifications for counseling approaches and foci.

Some characteristics of gifted adolescents are associated with an increased risk of suicide. Dixon and his colleagues (Dixon, Cross, Cook, & Scheckel, 1995) summarized the following characteristics that may put gifted adolescents at risk of suicide: unusual sensitivity and perfectionism (Delisle, 1986), isolation related to extreme introversion (Kaiser & Berndt, 1985), and overexcitabilities (heightened psychological or physiological sensitivities), as identified by Dabrowski (1964, 1972). According to Delisle (1986), there are four issues making gifted adolescents susceptible to suicide attempts: perfectionism, societal expectations to achieve, differential development of intellectual and social skills, and impotence to effect real-world change. These issues are plausible explanations for gifted students' susceptibility, but we must keep in mind that there is not direct evidence that they actually have a role in the suicidal behavior of gifted students.

PERSONALITY, GIFTED STUDENTS, AND SUICIDAL IDEATION

The connections between personality types and suicidal behavior are of interest to the gifted community for several reasons. Although there are no studies that clearly link giftedness to increased rates of suicide (Cross & Cross, 2017b), it is important that concerned adults remain vigilant, nonetheless. In a literature review, it was reported that half of gifted students express introverted tendencies (Sak, 2004). In a study of honors college students, we found nearly two thirds were significantly more introverted than the normative sample (Cross, Cross, Mammadov et al., 2017). Lester (2011) reviewed 43 studies including extraversion/introversion and suicidality, and reported that a majority (*n* = 23) found a positive association between introversion and suicidality. Street and Kromney (1994) have also implicated individuals with these personality characteristics who were involved in suicidal ideation or behavior. Not only does this indicate a potential higher risk among students with gifts and talents, it also suggests the possibility of other mental health concerns. Given that introversion is common among students who are gifted (Cross et al., 2002; Cross, Cross, Mammadov et al., 2017), there may be a high likelihood these students could experience more psychological distress and may, therefore, be candidates for depression and/or suicidal ideation screening. Combined, these studies suggest vigilance on our parts when we see high introversion among students with gifts and talents.

PSYCHOLOGICAL AUTOPSIES AMONG STUDENTS WITH GIFTS AND TALENTS WHO COMPLETED SUICIDE

Subsequent to the suicides at the Academy (see Chapter 1), three psychological autopsies were conducted. Psychological autopsy is a case study approach to research that was begun originally to determine equivocal deaths for insurance/legal purposes. This method draws its data from family, friends, and significant others; family doctors; school; and the home in terms of books, music, and so forth. Interviews, records, and observations are used to gather data. The approach attempts to paint as complete a picture of the life of the student as possible. It is slow and time consuming to conduct.

After the results of the three autopsies were published, Tracy was requested to conduct a fourth study of a gifted student who completed suicide in Vancouver. The results below represent the findings of the in-depth studies. Following this section is a comparison of the four psychological autopsies.

Commonalities With Adolescent Suicide in the General Population

The following commonalities were found between three of the subjects studied and adolescent suicide in the general population (Cross et al., 1996):

1. All subjects were adolescent Caucasian males.
2. All subjects manifested four emotional states:
    a. depression,
    b. anger,
    c. mood swings, and
    d. confusion about the future.

3. All manifested similar behaviors:
    a. poor impulse control, and
    b. substance use and abuse.

4. All manifested four relational difficulties:
    a. romantic relationship difficulties,
    b. self-esteem difficulties (either by exaggeration or self-condemnation),
    c. conflict-filled family relationships, and
    d. isolation from persons capable of disconfirming irrational logic.

5. The subjects shared warning signs in six categories:
    a. behavior problems,
    b. period of escalation of problems,
    c. constriction (including withdrawal from friends, dichotomous thinking),
    d. talking about suicide,
    e. changes in school performance, and
    f. family histories of psychological problems (p. 405).

COMMONALITIES AMONG THE THREE CASES RELATED TO THEIR GIFTEDNESS

The following were commonalities related to giftedness between the subjects studied (Cross et al., 1996):

1. The subjects exhibited overexcitabilities or heightened sensitivities:
    a. expressed in ways or levels beyond the norm even among their gifted peers;
    b. had minimal prosocial outlets;
    c. experienced difficulty separating fact from fiction, especially overidentification with negative asocial or aggressive characters or themes in books and movies;
    d. experienced intense emotions;
    e. felt conflicted, pained, and confused; and
    f. had difficulty with the role of emotions (e.g., one case devalued emotional experience, while two cases wanted to experience pain).

2. The subjects expressed polarized, hierarchical, egocentric value systems.
    a. The subjects engaged in group theoretical discussions of suicide as a viable and honorable solution.
    b. The subjects expressed behaviors consistent with Dabrowski's Level II or Level III of Positive Disintegration.
    c. The subjects attended residential school as a means of escape from their family or hometown. (p. 406)

In comparing the psychological autopsy of the three original intellectual gifted students who completed suicide with the fourth (Reed Ball), there were many similarities (Cross et al., 2002). Note that Reed's mother has requested that we always use his name during our research writing in lieu of traditional terms such as "subject," "client," "deceased," and the like. This is in an effort to enhance the cause of diminishing the stigma family members often feel after their loved one has completed suicide. The similarities found included (Cross et al., 2002):

1. All four subjects exhibited overexcitabilities. Their overexcitabilities were expressed in ways or levels beyond the norm even among their gifted peers. The four subjects had minimal prosocial outlets. All four subjects experienced difficulty separating facts from fiction, especially overidentification with negative asocial or aggressive characters or themes in books and movies. They experienced intense emotion, felt conflicted, and wanted to rid themselves of emotions.

2. Each of the young men expressed polarized, hierarchical, egocentric value systems.

3. They each engaged in group discussions of suicide as a viable and honorable solution.

4. Additionally, all four subjects expressed behaviors consistent with Dabrowski's Level II and Level III of Positive Disintegration. (p. 252)

There were also other similarities between the fourth student and the original three (Cross et al., 2002):

Reed was a Caucasian male who manifested four emotional characteristics: depression, anger (represented more in suppressed rage and frustration than physical actions), mood swings and confusion about the future, while demonstrating poor impulse control (manifested more often in patterns of thought more than behavior). He experienced three relational commonalities with those in the general population who complete suicide: romantic relationship difficulties, self-esteem difficulties (either by exaggeration or self condemnation), and isolation from persons capable of disconfirming irrational logic. Reed shared warning signs in several categories: behavior problems, period of escalation of problems, constriction, withdrawal from friends, dichotomous thinking, talking about suicide, and erratic school performance. (p. 252)

ADDITIONAL CASE STUDIES

Hyatt (2010) conducted a psychological autopsy of a highly gifted girl who died by suicide at age 18. "Amber" had experienced severe social isolation and her giftedness led to her being misunderstood by peers and adults. She mistrusted adults, including her parents, and exhibited significant self-oriented perfectionism. As in the four previous cases, Amber planned her suicide for several years, not hesitating to discuss it with her peers. She experienced similar emotional states and similar confusion about her future as the subjects in Tracy's studies (Cross et al., 1996; Cross et al., 2002). Implications Hyatt drew from her study included the need for measures to be taken to reduce bullying, for counseling of students with perfectionistic beliefs, and for adults to be educated on the social and emotional needs of gifted students.

Overexcitabilities similar to those seen in all of the psychological autopsies were observed in the gifted female subject of Peterson's (2014) longitudinal case study, who had expressed suicidal ideation in her teen years. Peterson saw evidence that her subject's giftedness served as a protective factor, particularly when she was able to analyze and problem solve in her own situation. Giftedness was also named as a protective factor by the gifted, gay subjects in Sedillo's (2015) study, all of whom had experienced suicidal ideation. Extensive descriptions of other cases of gifted individuals who died by suicide or considered it seriously have been published, but not as peer-reviewed research (e.g., Johnson, 1994; Peterson, 1993; Scheiber, 2013).

PERFECTIONISM

A number of studies of suicidal behavior among gifted students have found evidence of perfectionism as a contributing factor (Hyatt, 2010; Peterson, 2014; Sedillo, 2015; Seiden, 1966). The three dimensions of Hewitt and Flett's (1991) theory of perfectionism—self-oriented, other-oriented, and socially prescribed—have not been found to be equally influential in causing psychological distress. Whereas self- and other-oriented perfectionism have been associated with positive striving for excellence (Speirs Neumeister, 2015), high levels of socially prescribed perfectionism have been associated with more negative outcomes (Hewitt & Flett, 2004; Johnson, Panagioti, Bass, Ramsey, & Harrison, 2017; Stoeber & Otto, 2006). This tendency to believe that others have unrealistic expectations for one's perfect behaviors correlates with a host of negative psychological outcomes (Stoeber & Otto, 2006). In a model relating suicidal behaviors and social disconnection, Hewitt, Flett, Sherry, and Caelian (2006) included socially prescribed perfectionism as a potential factor. The presence of perfectionism in several of the studies cited here suggests it may be a significant factor in suicidal behavior among students with gifts and talents and warrants special attention.

CONCLUSIONS

Although drawing conclusions from such a small research base is risky, especially when dealing with suicide, a few important lessons can be noted. The research that compares data from students with gifts and talents with that from the general population is quite valuable. This gives us a practical tie to tried-and-true suicidal factors. In other words, predicting suicidal behavior among gifted students can be aided by research on the general population. Students with gifts and talents are in many ways the same as their average peers, and what little research has compared their suicide ideation has found no statistically significant difference. This indicates that research from the general population can inform our explorations. Exceptional abilities, however, alter the lived experience for these students and, quite possibly, the way they think about that experience and the possibility of suicide, itself. Risk factors may differ when they are experienced in the context of exceptional abilities. A second lesson represents areas that seemingly are specific to students who are gifted. For example, the descriptions of overexcitabilities in all of the psychological autopsies are believed by many to be unique among students with gifts and talents. Using Dabrowski's theory may afford suicidologists hints as to the more vulnerable among gifted students. It is critical that adults attend to the unique needs of this population, if we are to help them through difficult times.

KEY POINTS

❖ As a demographic group, students with gifts and talents are difficult to follow due to the differences in defining a gifted population.

❖ The rates of suicidal behavior of gifted and nongifted same-aged students are assumed to be quite similar unless empirically proven otherwise.

❖ Baker (1995) found that the incidence of depression and suicidal ideation was similar for both gifted and nongifted adolescents.

❖ When examining suicidal ideation among gifted adolescents, Cross et al. (2006) found that they did not exhibit heightened rates of suicidal ideation as compared to their nongifted peers.

❖ Certain characteristics, such as unusual sensitivity and perfectionism, isolation related to extreme introversion, and overexcitabilities, may put gifted adolescents at risk of suicide.

❖ Delisle (1986) defined four issues that make gifted adolescents susceptible to suicide attempts: perfectionism, societal expectations to achieve, differential development of intellectual and social skills, and impotence to effect real-world change.

❖ Due to the ability or inclination of gifted adolescents to think about suicide in a different way from their nongifted peers, typical intervention methods may be ineffective or inappropriate for suicidal gifted students (Cross, 2008).

❖ Cassady and Cross (2006) found that the factor structure of suicidal ideation in the gifted sample was different from the three-factor structure defined by Reynolds (1987) and included (a) wishes and plans, (b) morbid fixation, (c) social isolation, and (d) social impact. This should be taken into consideration when developing counseling approaches for students with gifts and talents.

❖ Highly introverted gifted students could experience more psychological distress, are more at-risk for suicidal ideation, and, therefore, require close attention.

❖ Psychological autopsy is a case study approach to research that attempts to paint as complete a picture of the life of the student who completed suicide as possible. It draws its data from the environment and people connected to the student, and is time consuming to conduct.

❖ Predicting suicidal behavior among students with gifts and talents can be aided by research on the general population.

CHAPTER 6

THE PERSONAL EXPERIENCE OF STUDENTS WITH GIFTS AND TALENTS

Research on the personal experience of students with gifts and talents is rich, but uneven. Coleman (2011) divided the most salient research in this area into three categories: lived experience, mixed messages, and stigma. He claimed that the three in concert make up the personal experience of gifted students (Coleman, 2011; Coleman & Cross, 2000). Personal experience becomes a very important factor when trying to understand the very complicated lives of students with gifts and talents (Coleman, Micko, & Cross, 2015). This also plays an important role in reconstructing the suicidal mind of this population.

This chapter exists in this book on suicide because we can better understand the suicidal mind if we can get at personal experience. To study personal experience, phenomenology is required. Phenomenology is based on important assumptions, including the assumption that lived experience (lifeworld or *lebenswelt*) exists prereflectively (Husserl, 1970). This means that our experiences as people exist before we attempt to recreate them by adding labels (selecting words) to describe them. The labeling step reflects a second-order recreation of the experience, not the actual experience, and is subject to other aspects of our being. Phenomenology attempts to gain access to the lived experience of people before they start trying to recreate it with language. From this type of research, phenomenologists claim to co-create with the participants the essential elements of lived experience. In the case of suicidal behavior, phenomenological study allows us to more fully understand the experiences and meaning that preceded the thinking about suicide (ideation) and attempts from their perspectives, not merely that of the researcher. This is consistent with Durkheim's (1951) claim that one type of extrasocial cause that influences the suicide rate is the "organic-psychic dispositions." This is also consistent with Shneidman's (1993) thinking, who, late in his career, began using increasingly phenomenologically oriented research techniques to understand suicidal behavior and specifically what preceded it. This ultimately led to his pursuit of the essential components of psychache—the central component to his theory of suicidal behavior. Other, more traditional forms of research are believed by phenomenologists to be more reflective of the researcher and his or her assumptions about what is being studied, rather than the actual phenomenon. Therefore, given the inherently primal nature of suicidal behavior, some suicidologists believe research into important aspects of the lives of suicidal people must be studied using phenomenology (Cross et al., 2002; Shneidman, 1993).

This chapter ties together the three aspects of the personal experience of students with gifts and talents that we have come to understand primarily through phenomenological research: lived experience, mixed messages, and stigma, enabling the reader to more fully understand the complex nature of the suicidal behavior of students who are gifted. From that understanding, preventing suicide becomes more feasible.

LIVED EXPERIENCE

Much of the lived experiences of people, including those who are gifted, are of a social nature and culturally situated. One's own experiences, thoughts, and feelings tend to take place in varying contexts. From being alone, to interacting with family, to attending church or school, these differing contexts tend to elicit differing experiences. Other variables, such as time in history, geographic differences, gender, ethnicity, and so forth also influence experiences. Moreover, *when* students with gifts and talents have specific experiences relative to their ages (e.g., at 6 years old vs. 12 years old) is important to the phenomenology of the experiences. To make this section germane given the nature of book, we will limit the discussion to the research base of gifted students over the past 25 years in the U.S., as related to school.

As a young gifted child grows, being identified as gifted or not being identified as gifted matters in his or her experiences. The experience of being known as gifted tends to have roles and expectations ascribed to it. Many of these roles and expectations would not be true for nonidentified or nongifted students. For example, Cross, Stewart, and Coleman (2003) described students who are gifted speaking out about their lives in school:

> They spoke of being embarrassed when held up as examples for other students; confused when students taunted them; and upset when told by the teacher that he or she was disappointed in them due to a test score, incorrectly answering a question in class, or any number of other "failures." (p. 4)

The expectations placed on our students with gifts and talents are perceived early and become a screen through which growing up is filtered. Many will become successful students while developing a passion for learning (Coleman, 2011). Some will underachieve and experience considerable disappointment from others. Some will internalize their value as directly reflective of their accomplishments in school. Still others will minimize the expectations of themselves relative to school and hold higher expectations for their work in their local communities. This type of commitment can be seen in myriad examples ranging from students who are active in church, gangs, or anything in between. In essence, the lived experience of gifted students establishes the foundations of the person's identity.

"Feeling different" is common among gifted students, as research from both qualitative and quantitative approaches has found (Coleman et al., 2015; Cross, Coleman, & Stewart, 1993). Feelings of differentness can result from their abilities or their motivation being different from peers. Gifted students are often passionate about learning and highly intrinsically motivated when the subject is their favorite topic and even when it is not (Coleman & Guo, 2013). This experience can set them apart from their peers, who may not be able to participate in the learning in the same way or who may not value the learning over other activities. The potential for rejection or being misunderstood by peers is greater for gifted students who exhibit different abilities and motivation for learning. More extreme differences are likely to be accompanied by stronger peer responses (Gross, 2003). Differentness of any kind can be the impetus for victimization. Gifted students have reported both being victimized and engaging in bullying behaviors (Peterson & Ray, 2006).

The lived experience of gifted students in a special school designed to address their academic and social needs differs greatly from those who attend a school that is focused on average students (Coleman et al., 2015). Schools that bring together large numbers of high-ability students offer more frequent opportunities for gifted students to find peers of similar ability level and those who are similarly motivated. When a school is unprepared for the child who is so eager to learn and capable of more than her or his peers, it can be a demotivating experience. Forced to wait for peers who have not "got it" yet, or for teachers who are occupied with the majority of average students, gifted students may succumb to boredom (Peine & Coleman, 2010). Years, or even an entire school career, without appropriate pacing or challenge can lead gifted students to drop out (Kanevsky & Keighley, 2003; Zabloski & Milacci, 2012). It is likely to also lead to depression among some gifted students (Cross & Cross, 2015a).

The gifted label can enhance self-esteem and offers distinct advantages to many gifted students, but it can also come at a cost (Coleman et al., 2015). For example, teachers may single students out as examples for their peers, a practice that can affect their relationships (J. Cross, 2015; Cross et al., 2003). The label impacts students' lived experiences, as they attempt to interpret the mixed messages they receive from peers and adults.

MIXED MESSAGES

I'm different you know; you show intelligence and you're outspoken, and people tend to isolate you and put a label on you. (Cross et al., 2003, p. 203)

Students who are gifted in Western societies grow up experiencing unique expressions of mixed messages. In many countries, giftedness itself is widely argued about, with little agreement as to its definition. Within professional organizations made up of educators, counselors, psychologists, and administrators, participants often maintain tacit definitions of giftedness based upon their involvement with gifted students. Even within families, there can quite often be wide variations of the definition and meaning of giftedness. Enduring topics such as elitism, or whether giftedness is merely an asset, engender considerable and often strongly held beliefs about giftedness. Longstanding models of schooling have historically been based on keeping children of similar ages together, thereby keeping children of similar intellectual capacity apart. This fact has contributed to concerns about the potential harm to children when certain gifted education recommendations are put into place, such as grade skipping, early admission, or any other recommendations for acceleration (Cross, Andersen, & Mammadov, 2015; Siegle, Wilson, & Little, 2013; Southern & Jones, 1991). Educational legislation such as the No Child Left Behind Act (NCLB) of 2001 and its 2015 successor, the Every Student Succeeds Act (ESSA) have forced school districts to focus their attention on students just within reach of a performance band, while paying increasingly less attention to those who have already surpassed that relatively low band of expectations. NCLB created conditions for an entire generation of students with gifts and talents that devalued their actual performance in school, especially if they demonstrated mastery of the minimum competency test. Ironically, in the first edition of their classic book that provides a critical view of our schools, Howley, Howley, and Pendarvis (1995, 2017), years before NCLB was implemented, concluded that many of the schools in the U.S. are actually anti-intellectual environments.

These mixed messages about intellectual achievement are not new. In 1954, the great anthropologist Margaret Mead wrote:

> [A]lthough happiness and success are often used interchangeably there is an increasing emphasis in American life on happiness, defined as "enjoying life, living among friends who live the same way I do," contrasted with success which takes too much out of you, kills you at forty, or "being a brain and missing all the fun." Any degree of outstanding success is represented as cutting one off from the group so that it becomes fashionable not to get better grades than the others, not to be too good, not to go up too fast. These pressures for keeping on all fours with one's classmates, neighbors, business associates, which are increasing in American life, tend to be particularly felt in the school age groups, especially in the case of the child who shows intellectual or artistic gifts. (p. 211)

Mead's description of the situation for gifted children in the 1950s is appropriate even today, when programming options for advanced learners are often considered elitist (Bain, Bliss, Choate, & Sager Brown, 2007), even by gifted students themselves (J. Cross, Cross, & Frazier, 2013). The opportunities to fulfill one's potential are limited in a society that frowns upon those with greater than average abilities.

As every culture creates expectations for its people based on gender, race, ethnicity, socioeconomic groupings, religion, and so forth, students who are gifted also must figure out what being a gifted student means. They learn of society members' prejudices, general expectations, and academic expectations. They must live within their family and community rules, while feeling pressure to live up to their potential. Each teacher has tacit assumptions about gifted students that will play out in the students' lives in real time. At the same time, students with gifts and talents, like all students, are developing as people and are dealing with psychosocial developmental issues such as making friends, dating, and so forth. The myriad mixed messages add considerable conflict to these issues.

A recent conflicting trend, the emphasis on increasing the number of students moving into science, technology, engineering, and math (STEM), adds further fuel to the mixed messages that these students receive. Over the past quarter century, the professional organizations in gifted education (National Association for Gifted Children, The Association for the Gifted) have emphasized a multitude of talent domains in which students can and should develop talent. The effects of the recent federal emphasis and considerable funding for students to pursue careers in STEM has narrowed considerably the options for gifted students and sent the message that other talent domains are less valued. These examples reflect the wide-ranging and deeply held philosophical differences of people in society that end up being internalized by gifted students. Because of this fact, and the need to exist socially in school, students with gifts and talents create coping strategies for navigating the social waters of family, school, and community (Coleman & Cross, 1988). Mixed messages can lead to confusion about how to pursue one's talents and, ultimately, who one can or "should" be.

STIGMA OF GIFTEDNESS

In 1985, Coleman developed a Stigma of Giftedness Paradigm (SGP) based on the classic book by Erving Goffman (1963) entitled *Stigma: Notes on the Management of Spoiled Identity*. Falk

(2001) claimed that there are two categories of stigma, existential and achieved. He defined existential stigma as

> stigma deriving from a condition which the target of the stigma either did not cause or over which he has little control. Achieved stigma is earned because of conduct and/or because they contributed heavily to attaining the stigma in question. (p. 11)

Existential stigma is the type of stigma that the SGP attempts to illustrate. To that end, the SGP has three tenets:

1. Students who are gifted want to have normal social interactions.
2. Gifted students discover that, when others learn of their giftedness, they will treat the gifted students differently.
3. They realize they can manage information about themselves that others are allowed to have.

Note that "normal" social interactions are idiosyncratic. Each person determines his or her own goal for what is normal. Introverts and extroverts may have very different ideas of what normal social interactions should be like. When others learn of one's giftedness, their different treatment may not be worse, merely different than it would have been, had this fact remained unknown. Families may be supporting the third tenet of information management when they teach their children to behave differently across settings, including sharing information about themselves judiciously.

Several studies based on the SGP (e.g., Coleman & Cross, 1988; Cross et al., 1993; Cross, Coleman, & Terhaar-Yonkers, 1991) have been conducted. Each study has demonstrated that students who are gifted and talented attend schools that are complicated social environments, so complicated that Tannenbaum (1983) opined:

> There is evidence to show that the gifted are influenced by their peers', parents' and teachers' feelings about their

abilities. If they are seen as mental freaks, unhealthy personalities, or eccentric simply because they are brainy or creative, many of them will avoid the stigma through conformity. Some would rather underachieve and be popular than achieve honor status and receive ostracism. (p. 466)

Research has documented that gifted students engage in myriad social coping strategies (Coleman & Cross, 1988; Cross et al., 1991; Cross et al., 1993; Cross & Swiatek, 2009) to exist comfortably in their school. The strategies reveal the concerns of the students relative to gaining the social interactions they desire. For example, students who are gifted tend to have one of three goals for their social lives while in school. Coleman and Cross (1988) created a Continuum of Visibility that illustrates the three goals: standing out, becoming invisible, and disidentifying. When students who are gifted desire to stand out, to be known as a gifted person, they engage in social coping behaviors that bring attention to themselves for their giftedness. To that end, they may answer numerous questions during a single class period, talk about their accomplishments or test scores or any of a large number of attention-getting behaviors, or dress the part of a scientist. Students with gifts and talents who desire to become invisible or to blend in may do so by wearing clothes that are common to their schoolmates, answer few questions during class, sit quietly, protect their successful test scores from the view of other students, and so forth. These behaviors keep them from standing out. The third group (disidentifiers) is not satisfied with standing out or blending in, they want to be disassociated with other gifted and talented students. To do so, they may hang around with other groups of students stereotyped to be made up of nongifted students. When students who are gifted describe this behavior, they will mention groups such as druggies, emos, skateboarders, and goths. These groups will vary across schools. The strategy is based on the student identifying, within the social milieu of the school, the groups that are stereotyped to be comprised of nongifted students. This is despite the fact that gifted students tend to exist in virtually all groups of any school. Some girls claimed that, as a strategy for disidentifying, they would go on a date with a boy thought to be "dumb." Other students go out for activities for which they have no talent. Students with gifts and talents have many social coping strategies, no matter to which of the three goals they aspire (standing out, blending in, or disidentifying).

Given the complicated social environments of our schools (which, in many cases, are anti-intellectual in nature), plus the pervasive mixed messages received, what are the effects on the thinking of students with gifts and talents? For example, how do these complicating factors affect their psychological well-being? How do they affect their behaviors? How might they contribute to the suicidal ideation of gifted students? How does the confluence of these variables and the characteristics of individual students who are gifted affect them as it pertains to suicidal behavior?

KEY POINTS

- ❖ The personal experience of students with gifts and talents is divided into three categories: lived experience, mixed messages, and stigma (Coleman, 2011). Studying these three aspects together will allow us to better understand the complex nature of gifted students' suicidal behavior and may help prevent suicide.

- ❖ When researching suicidal behavior of students, the phenomenological approach allows us to more fully understand the experiences and meaning that preceded the ideation and attempts from the students' perspectives.

- ❖ Much of the lived experiences of all adolescents, including those who are gifted, are of a social nature and culturally situated.

- ❖ The lived experience of students with gifts and talents establishes the foundations of the person's identity.

- ❖ National-level education legislation (NCLB and now ESSA) has created conditions for an entire generation of gifted students such that their actual performance in school was not valued, especially if they have demonstrated mastery of the minimum competency test.

- ❖ Students who are gifted must figure out what being a gifted student means in their society and culture: They must live by their family and societal rules, while at the same time living up to their potential.

- ❖ Gifted students create coping strategies in order to fit in and deal with a multitude of mixed messages.

- ❖ In 1985, Coleman developed a Stigma of Giftedness Paradigm and attempted to illustrate existential stigma (i.e., stigma derived from a condition that the target of the stigma either did not cause or over which he has little control).

- ❖ Coleman and Cross (1988) created a Continuum of Visibility that illustrates the three goals students who are gifted set for themselves as a way of coping with complex social lives while in school: standing out, blending in, and disidentifying.

CHAPTER 7

TOWARD A MODEL OF SUICIDAL BEHAVIOR FOR STUDENTS WITH GIFTS AND TALENTS

Over the years that Tracy has pondered the suicidal mind and behavior of students with gifts and talents, he has considered the traditional research about suicide of the general population. He has considered contextual and historical influences and, finally, the actual research on the suicide of students with gifts and talents. His research conducting psychological autopsies caused him to see developmental aspects of suicidal behavior and the need to investigate the essence of lived experience of the suicidal mind. Learning that Shneidman had come to a similar conclusion fairly late in his career, he gained the confidence to make these aspects foundational to a new model that applied to students with gifts and talents. Shneidman's (1993) work was most compelling in its rich description of the primal experience of psychache.

This synthesis of information has led to the development of the spiral model of the suicidal mind of gifted children and adolescents. The model attempts to build on both Shneidman's (1993) work and the STM by Stillion and McDowell (1996). Conceptually, combined with gifted-specific research and observations, these two theories provide a comprehensive foundation that has the benefits of both the empirically validated research reflecting the general population and the fine distinctions needed to anticipate and understand the suicidal mind of students with gifts and talents.

The spiral model of the suicidal mind of gifted children and adolescents will be described conceptually below and illustrated to assist with the explanations. It builds from the model categories and risk factors of the STM along with the more phenomenological aspects of Shneidman's (1993) theory, to the more nuanced, empirically based ideas from the research on suicidal behavior of gifted students. For context, however, before presenting the spiral model, we will provide a two-dimensional illustration of a triangle (see Figure 3) based on the Stillion and McDowell (1996) and Shneidman (1993) theories, plus the research about gifted students and suicide. Subsequently, we present the spiral model, which attempts to provide a three-dimensional image of the interactions of all of the factors provided to date, including those specific to students who are gifted.

The bottom fourth of the triangle includes the four categories of the suicide trajectory model (see Table 11, p. 34, for a reminder of what those categories entail). The correlates and risk factors of suicidal behavior establish the foundation of the suicidal mind. However, many people function well, even with many of the suicidal correlates.

The STM establishes an excellent foundation of risk factors from which to look for and predict suicidal behavior. The four categories are comprehensive, including biological traits/characteristics (e.g., being male), psychological characteristics (e.g., mood states), negative cognitive patterns (e.g., self-talk), and environmental factors (e.g., social isolation and exposure to lethal weapons). These factors are at a level that educators could be trained to identify as a means to reduce the likelihood of suicidal behavior.

The next level of the triangle includes factors identified from research on the suicidal behavior of students with gifts and talents. Isolation, feeling different, lived experience, mixed messages, and others are layered on top of the factors of the STM.

The third tier of the triangle includes the elements within Shneidman's (1993) theory. He described suicide as having four

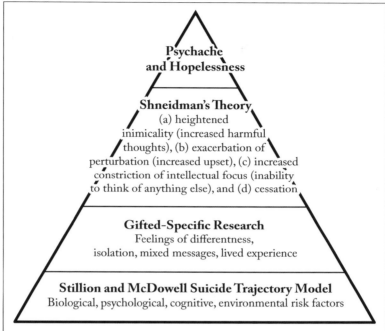

Figure 3. Illustration of suicide theories and students with gifts and talents leading to spiral model.

elements: (a) heightened inimicality, (b) exacerbation of perturbation, (c) increased constriction of intellectual focus, and (d) cessation. From the STM, we can now see how the process of the suicidal mind is becoming actively involved. As suicidal ideators increase their harmful thoughts and become more and more upset, they become less able to think about anything else. The only discernable solution is cessation: death. Factors associated with suicide can be considered kinetic, and Shneidman's theory illustrated how the factors become activated or engaged.

As the person becomes increasingly involved in suicidal ideation, the factors noted in the STM, such as rigidity of thought, exacerbate the perturbation (increase the upset) that Shneidman (1993) described. This is where the two most important states can have the effect of preparing the person to die: psychache and hopelessness. As a person experiences increasing amounts of psychological and emotional pain, the variable of hopelessness becomes more and more important.

Risk factors can be considered distally related to suicide, while warning signs such as psychache and hopelessness are thought to be proximally associated with a suicidal behavior and related to imminent risk. Distal causes are believed to be the initial causative factors in the original environment, while proximal causes are current causative factors.

These proximal causes can be seen at the top of the triangle, in Shneidman's (1993) psychache and the construct of hopelessness. The two states of mind are much closer to potential suicidal behavior than any of the correlates. However, the correlates provide fuel for the psychache that leads to hopelessness, which in turn leads to suicidal behavior.

SPIRAL MODEL OF THE SUICIDAL MIND OF GIFTED CHILDREN AND ADOLESCENTS

Building on the theories and research represented in the triangle in Figure 3, Tracy developed the spiral model of the suicidal mind of gifted children and adolescents, shown in Figure 4. The image of the spiral was chosen as a good metaphor for a person's life and how differing events, circumstances, and protective factors battle to keep a person spiraling high above the destruction on the ground before one crashes through and dies. The image allows for important details to be shown as weights or protective factors.

The swirling around at the top of the spiral illustrates the movement in one's life in a relatively flat plane of positive mental health. This is where most people operate on a day-to-day basis, when their lives are in a positive state. An individual's path dips with events and circumstances in life that cause high levels of upset, anxiety, or distress, but remains in a generally positive tra-

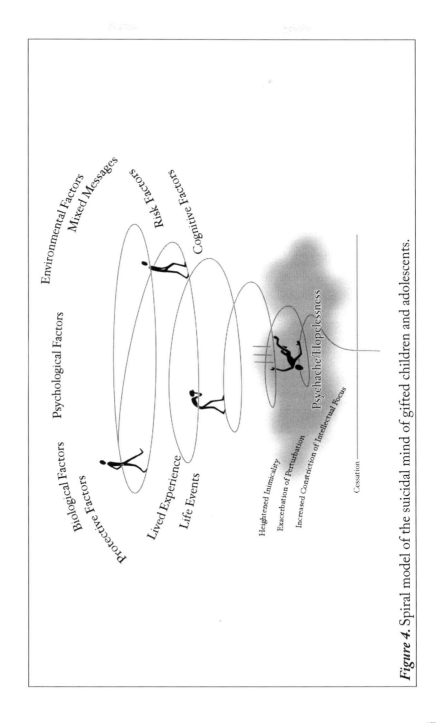

Figure 4. Spiral model of the suicidal mind of gifted children and adolescents.

jectory along the top. Negative effects on the mental health plane of the top spiral tend to be episodic for most people. Those people with bipolar disorder, for example, experience extreme emotional swings, and would reflect that in their image of the spiral, with many dips along the top plane. Others' patterns, while idiosyncratic, would tend to reflect a relatively consistent plane, indicating the ability to deal effectively with life's struggles.

Just as a tornado moves, a person is moving, developing over time. The height of the spiral is meant to reflect the distance one is from suicide, or, stated differently, a person's level of mental well-being. The width of the body of the spiral reveals the speed of life as one experiences it.

A way to imagine this is to assume that this model of mental health represents the life of a person across his or her lifespan. For some, the spiral lasts 85 years or more, while others die at birth. For those who survive birth, many of the protective factors are present, such as good health, positive parent-child relationship, and so forth. The image of a newborn actually illustrates the early indicators of the importance of relationships with others to the mental health of a person as he or she grows into adulthood. More specifically, if the child is not fed, then he or she dies. If he or she is not changed regularly or is neglected, then he or she fails to resolve a psychosocial crisis and develops doubt about how much trust can be placed in others (Erikson, 1963)—a doubt that is carried through life. As the young person develops, increasing numbers and types of protective factors are also developing. For example, love for family and friends, a sense of identity, development of agency, belief in one's competence, and many more are added to the biological predispositions that help keep a person safe. Belief systems that make suicide taboo can also be helpful in keeping people alive.

In sum, the spiral serves as a reasonable vehicle on which to place the numerous biological, psychological, cognitive, and environmental risk factors of Stillion and McDowell's (1996) theory. The same is true for Shneidman's (1993) psychological constructs of heightened inimicality, exacerbation of perturbation, increased constriction of intellectual focus, and cessation. Combined, these two theories establish a solid foundation to which we can add the gifted-specific issues, concerns, and phenomenological factors. In addition, Table 10 (see p. 27) provides a representation of both the factors associated with suicidal behavior and protections against it. If you consider it the backdrop for the spiral, it is easy to imagine how the person can be influenced over time.

The problem emerges when a person gets knocked out of his or her spiral that is parallel to the ground. Stillion and McDowell (1996) noted myriad life events that can cause this, such as divorce, moving, illness, death of family members, and relationship problems. Table 10 also includes some of the precipitating factors that can contribute to the drop off the top plane. In most cases, the protective factors such as those in Table 10 illustrate why we tend to bounce back, regaining our symmetrical orbit, parallel to and above the ground. Drugs and alcohol, depression, or other comorbid psychological issues are examples of factors associated with suicidal behavior. These can be seen in Stillion and McDowell's (1996) and Gould et al.'s (2003) work. As illustrative as these correlates and risk factors are, it takes hopelessness and Shneidman's (1993) psychache to break through the protective factors that keep us safe from suicide. The intense psychological pain and hopelessness make a person most susceptible to efforts at eliminating the overwhelming, inescapable pain. Suicide attempts are most likely to occur at this point.

The spiral, with the issues and factors from research on students with gifts and talents, provides a visual aid in understanding the suicidal mind of the child or adolescent. For example, we have learned that the factor structure of suicidal ideation among gifted adolescents is different from that of their nongifted peers (Cassady & Cross, 2006) and that gifted adolescents reveal some personality types (introversion and perceptive) that are more closely associated with suicidal ideation than the general population (Cross et al., 2006; Cross, Cross, Mammadov et al., 2017). Although these two examples are important, the research needs to be replicated with expanded samples of students with gifts and talents.

Research on the personal experience of giftedness suggests that gifted and talented students receive mixed messages abut their giftedness (Coleman & Cross, 1988), often grow up in anti-intellectual environments (Howley et al., 2017), believe that they are different from others (Cross et al., 1993), perceive a stigma of giftedness (Coleman, 1985), and engage in social coping behaviors (Coleman & Cross, 1988; Cross & Swiatek, 2009) to create a level of comfort within their schools. The internalization of these influences on the identity of gifted students adds to their negative self-images, inducing a lack of confidence and self-doubt. Moreover, the simple fact is that extraordinary minds have few peers. Combined, these factors can lead to anxiety, isolation, alienation, and depression—correlates of suicidal behavior. In the spiral model of suicidal behavior, we can see how the weight of negative correlates can hasten the downward progress toward a desire to end one's life and, then, to cessation. This progress may be halted and even reversed, when we bolster protective factors and attend to the contributing factors and predispositions through such practices as counseling, social work, or active engagement.

KEY POINTS

❖ The spiral model of the suicidal mind of gifted students builds from the model categories and risk factors of the Suicide Trajectory Model (STM) to the more phenomenological aspects of Shneidman's (1993) theory, to the more nuanced, empirically based ideas from the research on suicidal behavior of students with gifts and talents.

❖ The factors of the STM are generally at a conceptual level that professional educators could be trained to identify, and in many cases work with, to reduce the likelihood of suicidal behavior.

❖ The next level of the spiral model is Shneidman's (1993) theory, illustrating how the factors associated with suicide become activated or engaged.

❖ Risk factors can be considered distally related to suicide, while warning signs such as psychache and hopelessness are thought to be proximally associated with suicidal behavior and related to potential imminent risk.

❖ The weight of accumulated risk factors can make descent through the spiral faster. Protective factors enable upward movement and lend stability to an individual.

CHAPTER 8

PREVENTING SUICIDE AMONG STUDENTS WITH GIFTS AND TALENTS

A SCHOOL-BASED APPROACH

To help prevent the suicides of students with gifts and talents, our focus will be on the contribution that schools can make. The primary reason to focus on schools is because virtually all of these students attend schools and can be reached within this institution. A second reason for the school-based emphasis is the fact that schools have considerable resources to bring to bear. There is also the invaluable potential of peers and faculty and staff to provide important services on behalf of the potentially suicidal student. The final reason is that schools are replete with friendship groups. Other students often have information about a potentially suicidal student before the adults do. For a comprehensive system to be created, people in all of these roles must participate.

A number of school-based suicide prevention programs are available on the market (see Katz et al., 2013 for a review of 16 prevention programs). Prevention programs are intended to reduce the prevalence of all suicidal behaviors, from ideation to attempts and completions. Some programs approach this goal by enhancing awareness about suicide. This can be done with students and/or staff. Participants learn how to recognize the signs of distress and what to do when they are present. These programs can be very effective in getting students to the right helping resources, but are not aimed at reducing their suicidal ideation (Katz et al., 2013).

Few prevention programs have empirical evidence of their effectiveness, but there are some with a strong research base. One strongly supported program, *The Good Behavior Game* (GBG), significantly reduced suicidal ideation and attempts among nearly 2,000 high school students who had training 15 years earlier when they were in the first and second grade. By teaching students how to avoid engaging in aggressive and disruptive behavior at an early age, they were half as likely to experience suicide ideation and less likely to attempt suicide than students in the control group when they were 19 to 21 years old (Wilcox et al., 2008). Other prevention programs have a similar focus on helping students develop coping, problem-solving, and other life skills.

Based on our experience, we can make recommendations for how to create a customized approach to suicide prevention. To be most effective, schools need to create an overt, comprehensive plan for the entire school. Gifted students will benefit from a whole-school program that includes attention to their unique needs as one component. The plan should begin with a steering committee representing all of the stakeholders. As stakeholders themselves, older students may be included in the steering committee. Specific goals and objectives should be delineated that can be measured from year to year to prevent slippage with the influx of new students and changes in school personnel. As the example of the GBG program and our School-based Psychosocial Curriculum Model (SPCM; described in Chapter 9) suggest, effective supports can be developed at a very early age. A comprehensive plan can include elementary, middle, and high schools. The goals and objectives should be developmentally appropriate and should be established for each stakeholder group. Ideally, the suicide prevention plan would be a significant part of an overarching plan to create a *caring community*.

Caring communities attempt to help all students thrive in all aspects of their school lives. To begin, *thriving* must be defined. From its definition, indicators can be developed. For example, thriving might be defined as "students will demonstrate psychological well-being, appropriate levels of academic achievement, and reasonable levels of physical fitness." The metrics used to consider these areas would be both normative and idiosyncratic. Students should be measured against their school population (normative), but with consideration for individual differences (idiosyncratic). This guarantees both a sociological and individual perspective. Because suicidal behavior is predicted by environmental and phenomenological factors, both perspectives are needed to prevent it. Efforts to enhance the protective factors listed in Table 10 (see p. 27) will promote thriving among all students, including those with gifts and talents. All students can benefit from "individual coping, self-soothing and problem-solving skills," but providing an "appropriate academic challenge" will require special attention for gifted students. Even "interpersonal connectedness/belonging" can be a challenge for students who have few or no peers in the school with similar intellectual abilities or interests. In a caring community, all members will be concerned with the social and academic aspects of the environment that foster personal thriving.

To reach the goals and objectives established, information will have to be heard, understood, and internalized, and behaviors will have to be changed. To that end, significant ongoing training is required. Training should be tailored for the various stakeholder groups and at varying degrees of sophistication. For example, because everything planned would be under the goal of thriving, some specific knowledge about suicide (e.g., prevalence, risk factors, warning signs) would necessarily be included strategically for the greatest impact. Teachers, administrators, and counselors should receive an introduction to the unique experience of gifted students and how to meet their needs. Knowledge of their different lived experiences may make it easier to identify distress among students with gifts and talents.

In addition to the basic goals established to create a caring community in which everyone thrives, officials would also need to identify characteristics and expectations of the community. Some characteristics might include open communication, personal responsibility, community responsibility, candor, and no bullying. Another aspect of a caring community wherein everyone thrives is the inclusion of stakeholders across decision-making groups in an effort to share power. The most important outcome of embracing these community characteristics should be the creation of trust. Trust provides a guarantee that a caring community can exist and be maintained. An important underpinning of a caring community is that the adults will be appropriately trained to gain enough knowledge and expertise to provide the awareness, guidance, and decision making needed to create a safe, caring community. Good will, absent of significant training, can actually contribute to a less safe environment. For example, adults are prone to believe some of myths associated with suicide and gifted students (King, 1997), like those in Table 12. Many of these myths are widely held and assumed to be true for all students. These false beliefs can make it difficult to create a caring community wherein all students thrive. Education of the realities about suicide must be taught and school employees will need to be held accountable to know them.

An effective way to create comfort among educators relative to suicide is to address their self-imposed concerns on three fronts: (1) some educators believe that no student is serious about completing suicide, (2) some educators avoid any contact with the issue out of fear they are unprepared to make even the most elementary assessment of students being in distress, and (3) some educators believe that talking about suicide will increase the likelihood of it happening. One way to attend to all of these concerns/fears is to share with educators that they should not expect to operate as experts of suicidal behavior per se, as that is the domain of a clinical psychologist or psychiatrist (for the most part). Instead, their goal should be merely noticing students in distress. When they realize this is a more appropriate expectation for their involvement, educators tend to become willing to be part of a team that is trying to reduce suicidal behavior. Most educators develop an eye for noticing students in distress and the additional training helps them know how to expand their knowledge, while at the same time learning about additional steps they can take to be helpful.

Table 12
Common Myths Associated With Suicide and Gifted Students

Myth #1	Suicide occurs without warning.
Myth #2	Gifted and talented youths who talk about suicide are not serious about committing suicide.
Myth #3	Educating gifted students about suicide can lead to an increase in suicide ideation among this population coupled with more knowledge about ways of being successful in their suicide attempts.
Myth #4	If a gifted young person wants to commit suicide, very little can stop him or her.
Myth #5	Only trained counselors or mental health professionals are capable of intervening with suicidal gifted youths.

Many educators fear suicide to such an extent that they avoid getting involved. Others do not know what to do, and a small group worries about being made a fool by students trying to manipulate them. By emphasizing the goal of discerning distress in students, educators feel more comfortable and become more active in the process.

In a school-based suicide prevention program at the middle- and high-school level, educators and students would receive training in the basics about suicide, including its definition, prevalence rates, correlates, risk and protective factors, and so forth among the general population. Ideally, parents would be included, as well. School administrators and counselors would be trained in the most current knowledge about suicide and about students with gifts and talents. Teachers would receive important information about suicide, gifted students, and distress and what to do next. This information might emphasize how to identify distress and when and how to make referrals.

Other schoolwide information should include the importance of taking steps to help students in distress and the fact that suicide can be prevented, even among those who are already suicidal. In some cases, developing a positive mantra can be helpful. Tracy was part of a team that was able to initiate this change during the postvention subsequent to the three suicides of students involved with the Academy. He later directed the Academy and worked toward institutionalizing these important changes. He took his cues from the group most knowledgeable in schools about students in distress: the students. A cross-current that sometimes exists in schools is a belief among students that telling adults someone they know is struggling would be "ratting them out." In some environments, ratting a peer out to adults is to be avoided at all costs. The mantra that all students at his residential school heard was that it is better to have a live enemy than a dead friend (Cross et al., 1996). Adults often overlook students' awareness of their peers' emotional states. Consequently, including students in organizing and steering committees will help in the creation of effective communication processes that lead to trust. Without this element, the school environment may not be as safe.

Training to create a caring community includes an emphasis on the need for the school to be made up of people who see the value of helping the school reach the goals set for it. Of course, school goals can take many forms and cut across a large number of areas. For example, in addition to the mental health aspect of the school, academics, sports, and other extracurricular aspects of the school can be pursued. Nutrition and exercise are important to all of the aforementioned goals, but are seldom included in this process. As noted, an essential aspect to obtaining support across all groups is the inclusion of all groups in the process. Consequently, pulling everything under the diversity topic makes good sense here. Because schools tend to be microcosms of communities, they tend to reflect considerable diversity. When aspects of diversity that are salient in schools are added to the mix, the stakeholder groups should take on the form of the diversity represented. This inclusive practice bodes well for the creation of a caring community wherein trust is the defining characteristic. Facilitators are utilized to assist groups focusing on topics ranging from educational needs, to needs related to ethnicity, to mental health matters. All are respected as part of the community, and none are held in disdain, contempt, or fear. Implicit in a caring community is the need to also be a learning community. To function in the increasingly complicated world, it is essential that all parties continue their educations. This aspect of the caring community guarantees the trust and high levels of expertise needed to address serious problems such as preventing suicides. When an appreciation for the need for continuous learning is missing from the numerous aspects of the caring community described, suicide prevention is treated in a manner that tends to further isolate people while exacerbating distrust.

Several recommendations for an effective suicide prevention program involve modifications or additions to the school curriculum. Schools may wish to consider including a unit on suicide prevention as a part of the mental health curriculum, beginning as early as middle school. The mental health curriculum should consider strategies that incorporate common needs of students, including their need for acceptance, companionship, and self-understanding. Students play a crucial role in recognizing other adolescents who are suicidal (Delisle, 1990), and the more educated they are about suicide, the more of an asset they become. Eckert, Miller, DuPaul, and Riley-Tillman (2003) described curriculum programs for students that attempt to (a) heighten awareness regarding suicide, (b) train them to recognize signs of suicidal behavior in order to help others, and (c) provide students with information about various school and community resources. Although research suggests proceeding cautiously when implementing suicide curriculum programs, it has been shown to be an effective approach for intervening in school settings (Eckert et al., 2003).

Reynolds's model (as discussed in Eckert et al., 2003) includes a two-stage screening and assessment process. The process identifies potentially suicidal students and could be used as schoolwide practice for suicide prevention. In the first stage, a classwide or schoolwide screening takes place, in which all students complete a brief self-report measure to identify those who may be at risk for suicide. The second stage involves doing individual interviews with all students who score above clinically significant levels. This is where the expertise and manner of professional school counselors or psychologists can be very helpful. Although promising, screening is not 100% effective. Screening tools tend to report false positives for some young people while missing others who are at risk (Eckert et al., 2003). Consequently, educators are encouraged to employ a screening tool more than once.

Schools involved in suicide prevention should create an environment that promotes and reinforces positive social relationships (Fleith, 1998). In this setting, students feel comfortable sharing their concerns and are encouraged to dream and use their imaginations. In essence, according to Fleith (2001), schools should encourage activities that nurture students' interests, strengths, and abilities.

Suicidologists representing the dominant paradigm claim that suicidal behavior beyond ideation is not evidence of youths working through difficulties in their life. Rather, it is illustrative of people struggling with some form of mental illness (Pelkonen & Marttunen, 2003). This is an important consideration when deciding what facets to include in a schoolwide suicide prevention program (e.g., screening, counselor involvement, outside resources). School-based prevention programs risk alienating those students considering suicide by sending messages that can be misconstrued as equating suicidal ideation with mental illness. Ideation is quite common and widespread among people, while those actually attempting to take their own lives is a very small subset of the overall group of ideators. Consequently, while it is important to challenge students who engage in suicide ideation, it is also important not to conflate it with serious mental heath problems, as it may cause them to go underground and not pursue the help they need. On the other hand, describing suicide to students as a reasonable response to adolescent problems could inadvertently facilitate the expression of suicidal ideas. For this reason, educators must be aware of the potential to contribute to the idea that suicide is a viable option when experiencing stress. The myth that talking about suicide can promote suicidal behavior may have its roots in this delicate balance between trying not to paint students engaging in suicidal ideation as mentally ill, so as to support struggling students, while acknowledging the very real role of mental illness in actual attempts. These issues illustrate the importance of effective communication across the various stakeholder groups when implementing this type of school-based intervention.

The importance of creating a caring community in school cannot be overstated. In such an environment, myriad mental health issues are prevented, improved upon, and/or effectively monitored with the appropriate referrals made. The day-to-day activities of the stakeholders are carried out among community members who are dedicated to every person's wellness. People look after each other, feeling a personal responsibility. All stakeholder groups have considerable knowledge about distress, depression, frustration, and suicidal behavior. This type of environment creates protective factors that can help prevent suicidal behavior. In our opinion, *all* schools should create a caring community—the accumulation of benefits to the well-being of their students (and their faculty and staff) will be very important in enhancing positive mental health and, likely, academic success. To prevent suicides among students who are gifted, we must collaborate by drawing on the most up-to-date research available. This book can be used to begin the process of education about suicidal behavior in general and among our students with gifts and talents more specifically.

KEY POINTS

❖ Schools can help prevent the suicide of students for a number of reasons: virtually all students attend schools and can be reached within the institution; schools have considerable resources; schools have an invaluable potential of peers, faculty, and staff to provide important services on behalf of the potentially suicidal student; and schools are replete with friendship groups.

❖ School-based suicide prevention programs are available in the marketplace, with varying degrees of empirical support of their effectiveness.

❖ To be most effective, schools need to create an overt plan that includes a steering committee representing all of the stakeholders.

❖ Ideally, the suicide prevention plan would be a significant part of an overarching plan to create a caring community.

❖ Good will, absent of significant training, can actually contribute to a less safe environment, which is why adults in the caring community should be appropriately trained.

❖ One of the common myths associated with suicide and gifted students is that suicide occurs without warning.

❖ The realities about suicide must be taught and school employees will need to be held accountable to know them.

❖ An effective way to create comfort among educators relative to suicide is to reduce their self-imposed expectations that they need to be able to evaluate the potential for imminent harm. Instead, they need only to learn to recognize students' distress and how to respond.

❖ Including students in organizing and steering committees will help in the creation of effective communication processes and a safe school environment.

❖ It *is* better to have a live enemy than a dead friend.

❖ Schools may wish to consider including a unit on suicide prevention as a part of the mental health curriculum, beginning as early as middle school.

❖ Researchers and clinicians representing the dominant paradigm among suicidologists claim that suicidal behavior beyond ideation is not evidence of youths working through difficulties in their life, but of young people struggling with some form of mental illness.

❖ In a caring community, myriad mental health issues are prevented, improved upon, and effectively monitored with the appropriate referrals made.

❖ To prevent suicides among students who are gifted, we must collaborate by drawing on the most up-to-date research available.

CHAPTER 9

CREATING A POSITIVE ENVIRONMENT FOR STUDENTS WITH GIFTS AND TALENTS

In this section, we will consider what we know about the lived experiences of gifted students and how that knowledge can be put to use in helping them thrive psychologically in the school environment. There are unique factors that may increase protection or risk for these students, depending on how they are experienced in context.

When growing up gifted, there are several areas of development in which the gifted person's endogenous characteristics (those within the person) encounter the exogenous characteristics of differing environments. Some early examples include being an early reader, developing an impressive vocabulary, developing early advanced computer skills, beginning school early, and so forth. As very young gifted students encounter the norms among agemates, they often deviate from them, putting them at odds with the stereotypes and tacit values and, hence, the expectations of the other students and faculty. Consequently, depending upon the level of maturation of the gifted child's social cognition, he or she will begin the process of determining to what extent the school environment is supportive or hostile. In the mind of a young gifted child, he or she will not have the maturity that comes with experience and age to make informed decisions about complex social situations. This can cause young gifted children to internalize all sorts of mixed messages about giftedness and themselves, as described in Chapter 6.

As they progress in school, the degree to which the school environment is an anti-intellectual one will have an effect on gifted students' feelings of potential stigmatization. Many will develop social coping behaviors to try to create and maintain the social latitude they desire. The social coping behaviors can range from somewhat neutral behavior like sitting quietly, to underachieving. The net effect of experiencing mixed messages and anti-intellectual environments is the feeling of being different or aberrant.

When students with gifts and talents mature, being gifted is part of who they are as people. For many, it is very much a defining part of their identity. In schools that take academic matters seriously, they can thrive. Unfortunately, many of our schools are, in fact, anti-intellectual settings (Howley et al., 2017). It should be noted that the size of school matters here—larger urban and suburban schools create social environments that are not very porous. Moving between different social groups can be difficult, so many students with gifts and talents employ social coping strategies that can have negative impacts on their academic success. For example, underachievement or "going underground" can be the result of strategies for blending in or disidentifying.

Meanwhile, all of the typical developmental issues that affect school-aged children are also affecting gifted students. Giftedness becomes another way that the students appear nonmodal in the eyes of others, and in their own self-assessment. During adolescence, fitting in and standing out are often desired at the same time. Other examples of adolescent issues include wanting to be special while needing to feel the same as other students or feeling like one does not have any intellectual peers close to or the same as one's age. Because many schools seem to value sports more than academics, the groups with the lowest social status in many secondary schools are nonathletes who are studious (Brown & Steinberg, 1990; J. Cross, 2015; Tannenbaum, 1962). These examples make friendship formation difficult and often lead to limited prosocial outlets, a common finding in the psychological autopsies of gifted students who killed themselves (Cross et al., 2002).

It seems quite likely that the most pervasive threat to mental health of gifted students in school is the mismatch between the school's curriculum and the students' academic needs. Attending schools for years and constantly having this experience creates all sorts of problems for them. Although we have never actually seen a school that creates learning conditions wherein all students, including those who are gifted, operate at 100% capacity day in and day out, we estimate that many students who are gifted operate at less than 50% of their capacity for many years of their educational careers. This can be very frustrating for students with gifts and talents.

BUILDING A HEALTHY EGO

Over the years, we have created a number of recommendations that we believe help raise a well-adjusted gifted child (e.g., J. Cross & Cross, 2015b; Cross, 2017). At the center of many of our recommendations is Erik Erikson's (1963) Theory of Psychosocial Development. This theory offers a powerful explanation for the influence of childhood experience on later psychological functioning. Not only is it useful for parents to consider as they attempt to support their child's developing ego, Erikson's theory can also help to address psychosocial development in the later years. We have created a School-based Psychosocial Curriculum Model (SPCM; Cross & Cross, 2017a; Cross, Cross, & Andersen, 2017) based on Erikson's theory that may be used to help in the positive psychological development of students with gifts and talents. The likelihood of suicidal behaviors is reduced when these students have the psychological resources that come from a strong ego.

According to Erikson's (1963) theory, all people go through psychological crises, which come about as their physiology and psychological awareness comes into conflict with their environment. These crises arise in stages, with knowledge about oneself and the social world accumulating across the lifespan (see Table 13). Successful negotiation of the crisis results in a "favorable ratio" (Erikson, 1963, p. 271), between the opposing forces of the crisis. What is learned in each stage is not concrete and the beliefs one has acquired may be re-examined at any age. For this reason, our SPCM recommends lessons suggested by Erikson's stages and research on gifted students.

A brief primer on Erikson's stages gives an indication of the supports that are necessary for developing a healthy ego. The first crisis is *Trust vs. Mistrust* and it occurs in the first year of life. Newborns have needs that must be fulfilled by their environment. They need to eat and be changed in predictable ways, and they need affectionate human bonds. These experiences will help them build a basic trust in the world. From this they will develop hope for the future. Gifted students who have the essential strength of hope will trust their peers and teachers to have their best interest at heart. Such beliefs may be challenged when they receive mixed messages about their exceptional abilities. Some gifted students may mistrust others, assuming they do not have the student's best interest in mind with their demands. A little of both trust and mistrust will support the student's self-advocacy.

During the second stage of *Autonomy vs. Shame and Doubt* (about 1–3 years of age), children are ready to explore their surroundings. If they are unsuccessful due to interference from others, they may develop a sense of shame and doubt in their abilities to act on their own desires. It is no coincidence that the word most reflective of the terrible twos is "No," coming from both the child and the caregiver. Too many nos, however, can make the child doubtful of his or her ability to act in any way. The successful negotiation of this stage results in willpower. In the next stage of *Initiative vs. Guilt* (about 3–6 years of age), children move from simply acting to creating plans and then carrying them out. Their imagination allows for all sorts of creative endeavors, but the environment will not always allow these to come to fruition. Their planning often involves others—playmates, siblings, parents—who can help or hinder their success. Frequent frustration

Table 13
Erikson's (1963) Theory of Psychosocial
Development Stages of Crisis

Age	Crisis to be resolved	Virtue
Birth to 1 year	Trust vs. Mistrust	Hope
1 to 3 years	Autonomy vs. Shame and Doubt	Will
3 to 6 years (Pre-K–1)	Initiative vs. Guilt	Purpose
6 to 12 years (grades 1–6)	Industry vs. Inferiority	Competence
12 to 20 years (grades 7+)	Identity vs. Role Confusion	Fidelity
20 to 40 years	Intimacy vs. Isolation	Love
40 to 65 years	Generativity vs. Stagnation	Care
65 and older	Integrity vs. Despair	Wisdom

can lead to feelings of guilt. Always bending others to one's will can lead to the opposite—a sense of entitlement or belief in their power over others. Erikson (1963) would recommend a favorable ratio of initiative and guilt. The outcome of this crisis is a sense of purpose. Preschool can contribute greatly to a child's willingness and ability to take initiative in pursuing the plans they create. The timid gifted student may need encouragement to act on his or her own and the overdemanding gifted student may need lessons in perspective-taking and delaying gratification.

Children need to have success in school activities to develop a sense of competence. To that end, schools are key in providing opportunities for learned skills and productivity for elementary-aged children. During the next crisis of *Industry vs. Inferiority* (about ages 6–12), children are learning to use the tools that will be valuable to them in adulthood. They need opportunities to prove themselves capable of doing valued activities. In schools, this means they need practice with reading, analyzing, and experimenting. They must have *real* challenge, too. Erikson (1950/1980) wrote, "Children cannot be fooled by empty praise and condescending encouragement. . . . Their accruing ego identity gains real strength only from wholehearted and consistent recognition of real accomplishment, that is, achievement that has meaning in their culture" (p. 95). If they find they are not capable or are not able to test their abilities, they can develop feelings of inferiority. Too much or too little confidence in one's abilities will not lead to a healthy ego. Attending a school that does not provide gifted students with an appropriate curriculum may be damaging to one's developing ego. Especially in the later elementary years, these students need a match between their abilities and the curriculum.

In the crisis of *Identity vs. Role Confusion* (approximately ages 12–20), adolescents are coming to terms with the person they are and the person they want to be. All the stages before have led them to a recognition of their self in the world, with varying degrees of hope, willpower, purpose, and competence to inform their self-concepts. The early adolescent may explore different identities, trying on new looks, new activities, and new behaviors, just to see how they fit. In the 21st century, this task is extending further into adulthood than it did in Erikson's day. Adolescents need opportunities to see many admirable adults in various roles during this stage and gifted students need opportunities to explore the possibilities open to them, while still respecting their talents. Successful resolution of this crisis would be a sense of fidelity, of "sameness" between one's self-concept and how one perceives others to believe he or she is.

In the last stage appropriate for this book, *Intimacy vs. Isolation* (about ages 20-40), young adults need to develop loving relationships. Being willing to sacrifice one's time and resources for a passion—be it a person, a talent area, or an institution, for example—is an important psychosocial development. Not successfully negotiating this crisis leaves the person feeling isolated. Gifted students and those who work with and care for them need a realistic understanding of the sacrifices required for their talent development. The cost to parents may be great, but it is not the same as it is for the child.

Healthy egos result when people are hopeful that the environment will provide for them, but are not Pollyanna-ish in expectations that it will; when they believe in their ability to act, but are aware of the need to suppress actions that would negatively impinge on others; when they recognize what is possible *and* what is realistic; when they are confident, but not overconfident in their abilities; when they feel comfortable with their sense of self; and when they are able to make the sacrifices needed to develop a loving relationship with a person and/or a talent domain.

Parents of young children can consider Erikson's crises as their children are growing up, but those who are reading this book may be well beyond this part of their child's development. Counselors are familiar with the topic, however. We will discuss this more in Chapter 10. In schools that are concerned about supporting students' mental health, psychosocial curricula can be implemented. The SPCM (Cross & Cross, 2017a; Cross, Cross, & Andersen, 2017) can be used to design lessons that address the different crises. For example, issues related to hope can be addressed through lessons in recognizing internal and external resources or self-soothing skill development. By considering how the crises involve the self and others, particularly for gifted students in context, lessons can be created to bolster students' ego strength. Such curriculum may make its way into gifted programs, as we have learned that psychological health is a critical component of talent development (Subotnik, Olszewski-Kubilius, & Worrell, 2011).

Providing Psychological Support

In concert with the strong foundation guided by the work of Erikson, we should be able to help gifted children develop into well-adjusted adults, virtually free from suicidal behavior. Of course, we cannot prevent the correlates of suicide outside of the development of the individual gifted child. For example, a family member of a gifted child could complete suicide. This event can be a precipitating factor (see Table 10, p. 27) to suicidal behavior, but positive psychosocial development may be the protective factor that keeps this gifted student from descending from the top of the spiral. Included in the fifth edition of Tracy's book entitled *On the Social and Emotional Lives of Gifted Students* (Cross, 2017) are ideas for effective parenting, teaching, and guidance of students with gifts and talents.

All gifted students should participate from time to time in counseling. Most of the counseling will be educative—teaching prosocial skills, communication skills, how to deal with frustration and stress, and how to wait while other students catch up. Students can learn about what it means to be a gifted student and how hard work and practice are required to develop their potentials into specific talent domains. In secondary school, they will need considerable college and career counseling. In addition to emphasizing college and career counseling, they will also benefit from having opportunities to discuss friendships and other important relationships. This connection with a well-trained counselor or psychologist will ease the struggle of growing up gifted in our anti-intellectual culture. More serious problems can be identified early and dealt with before they become too serious.

Experience tells us that students with gifts and talents must spend some time together. The amount of time that is ideal is unclear, but time together helps with the feelings of being different that can be troubling during secondary school. Time in summer residential programs can be especially helpful in developing a positive self-concept and possible friendships. The cost of many such programs can be prohibitive, but scholarships may be available. The Internet also provides opportunities to connect students with others who have similar interests. These others may not be the same age as the student. It is imperative that online relationships be monitored carefully. Carefully cultivating appropriate relationships with someone who "gets" a student with gifts and talents, whether a same- or different-aged person, can result in rewarding psychological connectedness that may not be possible in one's school, community, or even family.

KEY POINTS

❖ Due to their endogenous characteristics, gifted students encounter challenges to norms early, and often find themselves in complex social situations.

❖ Gifted students often develop social coping behaviors to protect themselves from mixed messages or anti-intellectual environments.

❖ Some social coping strategies, such as underachievement or going underground, can have negative impacts on students' academic success.

❖ During adolescence, fitting in and standing out are often desired at the same time.

❖ The most pervasive threat to mental health of gifted students in school is the mismatch between the school's curriculum and the students' academic needs. As a result, many gifted students operate at less than 50% of their capacity, causing frustration and other problems.

❖ Erik Erikson's (1963) Theory of Psychosocial Development provides the age ranges at which differing crises must be resolved successfully to develop a healthy ego.

❖ Preschools can contribute greatly to development of the sense of purpose in 3–6-year-olds by helping them to successfully internalize initiative and some control in their lives.

❖ Schools play a key role in providing opportunities for learned skills and productivity, and can offer possibilities for success in school activities to develop industriousness.

❖ Although we cannot prevent the correlates of suicide outside of the development of the individual gifted child, we can provide helpful ideas and guidelines for effective parenting and teaching of gifted students.

❖ All gifted students should participate in counseling, where they can learn about what it means to be gifted, discuss friendships and other important relationships, and receive college and career advice. Counseling will also provide a chance to identify and work through more serious problems at an early stage.

❖ When teachers, counselors, and parents work together on the prevention of suicidal behavior of students with gifts and talents, the odds improve dramatically.

CHAPTER 10

MENTAL HEALTH SUPPORT FOR DISTRESSED STUDENTS WITH GIFTS AND TALENTS

Healing a suicidal mind is very difficult and not always successful. It requires considerable expertise in psychology or psychiatry. Consequently, it is not appropriate to include actual counseling advice here per se, as this book is for the general public and its readers are not expected to have the training required. Teachers, administrators, parents, fellow students, and even most school counselors should not be considering how to counsel a suicidal student with gifts and talents, but how to direct that student to professionals who can help. There are myriad factors that influence the potential for success in turning around a mind bent on suicide. Some of these include access to mental health professionals and the type and degree of comorbid factors. When a person is identified as potentially suicidal, assessing his or her risk of imminent harm is often the first step of treatment. The goal for assisting a person believed to be at this level of distress is simple and direct: keep him or her alive. Typically this leads to in-house care at a residential facility that specializes in serious mental health care. Those admitted often stay for 48–72 hours. They must be reevaluated for the potential of imminent harm before they can be released. In a perfect world, they remain as an outpatient, receiving appropriate psychological care on an outpatient basis. The treatment often includes both talk and potentially pharmaceutical therapy. Psychologists tend to provide the talk therapy while psychiatrists arrange the medications. Psychiatrists sometimes offer both services. Other combinations can also exist, such as clinical social workers, or other professionals licensed at the master's degree level who are supervised by licensed doctoral-level psychologists or psychiatrists. Specific techniques for therapy will vary based on the philosophical underpinnings of the training received by the psychologist providing the therapy.

Once the person is out of imminent harm, or if he or she was never in imminent harm, the most highly recommended approach includes both counseling and medication (if called for). One without the other, when both are recommended, is believed to be an inferior approach to treatment. Although describing a typical acute care medical model of healing a suicidal mind is important, this task is out of the hands of those who work in schools. Moreover, care after a person has been suicidal is inherently ameliorative. Much of this work is best done by highly trained professionals.

In the Presence of a Potentially Suicidal Individual

We know that a person in imminent danger of harming him- or herself should be placed in the care of professionals. Once a person is identified as suicidal and receiving appropriate psychological care, he or she should be among the professionals who can save him or her in the short term and help make the move from suicidal to stable. But many of the situations in which those of us who work or live with gifted students find ourselves are more ambiguous. How does a teacher who spots a student whose work is laced with death-related images or who appears self-loathing respond? When is it time to seek support from a professional? How does one act in the moment when faced with a depressed child? How can we create an environment that supports positive development, so the pain of psychache never enters?

To foster an environment where psychache does not emerge, adults must be on the lookout for students in psychological pain. As the spiral model illustrates, adults should be wary of life events that can throw their students with gifts and talents off the plane of positive mental functioning. Transition points, such as a move from elementary to middle school or middle school to high school, family moves that result in many changes, divorce, and death of a loved one (even a pet) are all precipitating events that can upset the balance on the plane of positive function. Those with predisposing or contributing factors (see Table 10, p. 27) should receive special attention. Adolescents who have made previous attempts or those who have poor coping skills may not be able to hoist themselves up from the lower levels of the spiral. Adults and peers can provide the support that is required, but concern for the individual is a necessary ingredient for success. A second ingredient is knowledge about what to do. It is important not to minimize students' reaction to a situation. Their perspective must be taken seriously, or they will not feel supported. It can help to work on their perceptions of a situation, but an adult's belief in the insignificance of the problem will not be helpful in doing so.

Peers can be a primary source of support, but it is extremely important to help them recognize their limitations. It is unfair to burden a peer with the responsibility of keeping a friend from falling into hopelessness. The responsibility he or she feels for the life of a peer is likely to go far beyond what an adult would feel. In order to respond appropriately, young people and adults alike must have proper education. What should someone say to a friend who expresses suicidal thoughts? When is it necessary to bring an adult into the situation? What adult is the right one? All schools should have at least one contact person who is available, sympathetic, and trusted by students and educated in the steps to take in the case of a suicidal child. All adults, including parents, should be trained in appropriate interventions—how to recognize a suicidal student, what to say, who to report it to, and when to report it. No one can be apathetic, or the student's slide down the spiral will continue unimpeded.

If teachers, counselors, parents, and administrators work together on the prevention of suicidal behavior of students with gifts and talents, the odds improve dramatically. Others, such as psychologists and psychiatrists are available, should the more proactive measures taken give way to bad experiences, changes in brain physiology, suicidal correlates, or traumatic events that can accumulate to move a person downward on the spiral model of the suicidal mind of gifted children and adolescents. Should that occur, all of the adults and fellow students should be prepared to play their respective roles to help the student in distress. With sufficient training, we can create a formidable team to prevent suicidal behavior and lend our support to the healing of the suicidal mind of gifted children and adolescents.

The role of a caring community is to establish a safe haven for students, teachers, counselors, and administrators. By creating a caring community, all of the stakeholders are trained on steps to take to keep a watchful eye for those in need of assistance. We believe that it is important to include the salient information about the unique aspects of the lived experience of gifted students in the training of the stakeholders in the caring communities. This allows for idiosyncratic developmental patterns of gifted students to inform the stakeholder practices. This would include identifying early evidence of distress and bringing appropriate resources to bear to keep potential significant problems from emerging. Should a student get to a place of significant distress, stakeholders in caring communities know how to bring the person in need—both figuratively and literally—to the appropriate designated professional who can provide the next level of care. At this point, the training allows appropriate decisions to be made as to whether a referral is needed. In short, our best chance at helping gifted students relative to suicidal behavior is to try to prevent it from occurring. This includes ideation, attempts, and completions. To that end we must learn about suicide, including its manifestations, patterns, correlates, and factors. We need to keep an eye out for students in distress and know what depression and anxiety look like in school-aged children. We need to understand that suicidal behavior has a primacy of experience that we may never have experienced ourselves. We need to understand psychache and hopelessness. We need to stay vigilant and be willing to act. We need to have the confidence to know that we will not cause a suicide, and we may be able to prevent one. When in doubt, do something (Cross et al., 1996)!

KEY POINTS

❖ School-based stakeholder groups (teachers, counselors, administrators, parents) can be the first line of defense in suicide prevention efforts.

❖ Only suitably trained counselors, clinical social workers, psychologists, and psychiatrists can give effective psychological support to gifted students who are suicidal.

❖ The appropriate role for teachers, administrators, parents, fellow students, and even most school counselors in the company of a potentially suicidal student is one of caring supporter who can guide her or him to trained professionals.

❖ A proper referral is quite often the most appropriate step to take to prevent a suicide attempt.

❖ Preventing suicidal behavior is the most effective approach to keeping students alive.

❖ Adults should be on the lookout for students in psychological pain, especially when they have experienced major life events, such as transition points in school or the death of a family member or pet.

❖ Schools can create caring communities that can be a robust defense against suicidal behavior.

RESOURCES

NATIONAL RESOURCES

INSTITUTE FOR RESEARCH ON THE SUICIDE OF GIFTED STUDENTS

The Institute exists as a research center focused on the suicidal behavior of gifted students. It serves as a clearinghouse of research and other salient information, designs and conducts research, and provides training on suicide prevention.

Center for Gifted Education
School of Education
William & Mary
301 West Monticello
Williamsburg, VA 23186

NATIONAL SUICIDE PREVENTION LIFELINE

This is a 24-hour, toll-free, confidential suicide prevention lifeline and online chat site for people in crisis. Calls are routed to the nearest crisis center in the national network of more than 150 crisis centers. The lifeline provides counseling and mental health referrals.

Hotline: 800-273-8255
Website: https://www.suicidepreventionlifeline.org
Facebook: https://www.facebook.com/800273TALK
Twitter: @800273TALK
YouTube: https://www.youtube.com/user/800273TALK

Online chat: http://suicidepreventionlifeline.org/GetHelp/
LifelineChat.aspx
You Matter Website: http://www.youmatter.
suicidepreventionlifeline.org

KRISTIN BROOKS HOPE CENTER

This is a not-for-profit organization that focuses on suicide prevention, awareness, and education. It provides help and hope through crisis hotlines, online crisis chat, and college campus awareness events.

Address: 1250 24th St. NW, Ste. 300, Washington, DC
20037
Website: http://hopeline.com
Hotline 1: 800-442-HOPE
Hotline 2: 800-784-2433 or 800-SUICIDA (Spanish)
Teen to teen peer counseling hotline: 877-968-8454 or
877-YOUTHLINE
Online Crisis Network: http://www.IMAlive.org
Online chat crisis support: https://www.imalive.org/chat.
php

JED FOUNDATION

A national organization that works to prevent suicide and promote emotional health among college and university students, the Jed Foundation also supports a student program, "Half of Us." This is a national campaign to raise awareness about mental health issues on campus and to connect students to resources to get help. The organization also has partnered with MTV to produce features in which artists discuss their own struggles with mental health issues.

Address: 6 E. 39th St., Ste. 1204, New York, NY 10016
Phone: 212-647-7544
Fax: 212-647-7542
Website: http://www.jedfoundation.org/students or http://
www.halfofus.com

THE TREVOR PROJECT

This resource is targeted at LGBTQ youth to provide crisis intervention, a digital community, and advocacy programs. The organization also sponsors several other resources for youth, including Ask Trevor, an online question and answer resource for youths looking for information and guidance on sexual orientation and gender identity; TrevorChat, a confidential, secure, and free online messaging service that gives live help to students not at risk for suicide; and TrevorSpace, an online social networking community for LGBTQ youths (ages 13–24) and their friends/allies.

Address: P.O. Box 69232, West Hollywood, CA 90069
Hotline: 866-488-7386
Los Angeles Office Phone: 310-271-8845
New York Office Phone: 212-695-8650
Fax: 310-271-8846
Website: http://www.thetrevorproject.org
Ask for Help Website: http://www.thetrevorproject.org/site/AskforHelp
TrevorChat Website: http://www.thetrevorproject.org/Programs
TrevorSpace Website: http://trevorspace.org
Facebook: https://www.facebook.com/TheTrevorProject
Twitter: @trevorproject
YouTube: https://www.youtube.com/thetrevorproject

STATE/LOCAL RESOURCES

ALABAMA

Crisis Center
Address: 3600 8th Avenue South, Ste. 501, Birmingham, AL, 35222
Hotline: 800-273-8255
Phone: 205-323-7777

Fax: 205-328-6225
Website: http://www.crisiscenterbham.com

ALASKA

Careline Crisis Intervention
Address: 726 26th Avenue, Ste. 1, Fairbanks, AK 99701
Hotline 1: 877-266-4357
Hotline 2: 800-273-8255
Phone: 907-452-2771
Fax: 907-457-2442
Website: http://www.carelinealaska.com

ARIZONA

EMPACT Suicide Prevention Center
Address: 618 S. Madison Dr., Tempe, AZ 85281
Hotline: 480-784-1500
Phone: 480-784-1514
Website: http://www.empact-spc.com

ARKANSAS

Arkansas Crisis Center
Address: 14 E. Emma, Ste. 213, Springdale, AR 72764
Hotline: 888-CRISIS2
Phone: 479-365-2140
Website: http://www.arcrisis.org

CALIFORNIA

WellSpace Health
Address: 1820 J St., Sacramento, CA 95811
Hotline 1: 916-368-3111
Hotline 2: 800-273-8255
Phone: 916-737-5555

Website: https://www.wellspacehealth.org/services/
counseling-prevention/suicide-prevention
Facebook: https://www.facebook.com/WellSpaceHealth
Twitter: @WellSpaceHealth

San Francisco Suicide Prevention
Address: P.O. Box 191350, San Francisco, CA, 94119-1350
Hotline: 415-781-0500
Phone: 415-984-1900
Fax: 415-227-0247
Website: http://www.sfsuicide.org
Facebook: https://www.facebook.com/sfsuicideprevention
Twitter: @SFSuicide

COLORADO

Metro Crisis Services, Inc.
Address: P.O. Box 460695, Denver, CO 80246
Hotline: 844-493-8255
Website: http://www.metrocrisisservices.org

CONNECTICUT

Department of Mental Health & Addiction Services
Address: 410 Capitol Avenue, P.O. Box 341431, Hartford,
CT 06134
Hotline: 800-273-8255
Phone: 860-418-7000
Website: http://www.ct.gov/dmhas/cwp/view.asp?q=335132

DELAWARE

ContactLifeline
Hotline: 800-262-9800
Website: http://www.contactlifeline.org

In New Castle County
Address: P.O. Box 9525, Wilmington, DE 19809
Hotline: 302-761-9100
Hotline TDD: 302-761-9700
Fax: 302-761-4280

In Kent and Sussex Counties
Address: P.O. Box 61, Milford, DE 19963
Phone: 302-422-1154
Fax: 302-422-2078

DISTRICT OF COLUMBIA

DC Department of Behavioral Health
Address: 64 New York Avenue NE, 3rd Floor, Washington, DC 20002
Hotline: 800-273-8255
Phone: 202-673-2200
Fax: 202-673-3433
Website: https://dbh.dc.gov

FLORIDA

Florida Suicide Prevention Coalition
Hotline: 800-273-8255
Website: http://www.floridasuicideprevention.org
Facebook: https://www.facebook.com/floridasuicidepreventioncoal

GEORGIA

Behavioral Health Link
Hotline: 800-715-4225
Phone: 404-420-3202
Website: http://www.behavioralhealthlink.com

Hawaii

ACCESS Line
Address: 1250 Punchbowl St., Room #256 Honolulu, HI
96813
Hotline: 808-832-3100
Phone: 800-753-6879
Fax: 808-586-4745
Website: http://health.hawaii.gov/amhd

Illinois

Community Counseling Centers of Chicago
Address: 4740 N. Clark St., Chicago, IL 60640
Phone: 773-769-0205
Website: http://www.c4chicago.org

Memorial Behavioral Health
Address: 710 N. Eighth St., Springfield, IL 62702-6395
Hotline: 800-273-8255
Phone: 217-525-1064
Fax: 217-525-9047
Website: https://www.memorialbehavioralhealth.org

Indiana

Mental Health American in Greater Indianapolis
Address: 615 N. Alabama St., Ste. 320, Indianapolis, IN
46205
Hotline: 317-251-7575 or text CSIS to 839863
Phone: 317-634-6341
Fax: 317-464-9575
Website: http://www.familiesfirstindiana.org

Iowa

The Crisis Center of Johnson County
Address: 1121 Gilbert Court, Iowa City, IA 52240-4528

Hotline: 319-351-0140
Phone: 319-351-2726
Fax: 319-351-4671
Website: http://jccrisiscenter.org

KANSAS

Headquarters Counseling Center
Address: 200 E. 8th, Ste. C, Lawrence, KS 66044
Hotline: 785-841-2345
Website: http://www.headquarterscounselingcenter.org

KENTUCKY

Crisis and Information Center, Seven Counties Service
Address: 10101 Linn Station Rd., Louisville, KY 40223
Adult Crisis Hotline 1: 502-589-4313
Adult Crisis Hotline 2: 800-221-0446
Child Crisis Hotline 1: 502-589-8070
Child Crisis Hotline 2: 800-432-4510
Phone: 502-589-1100
Fax: 502-589-8614
Website: http://centerstoneky.org

LOUISIANA

Crisis Intervention Center
Address: 4837 Revere Avenue, Baton Rouge, LA 70808
Hotline 1: 2-1-1
Hotline 2: 225-924-3900
Hotline 3: 800-437-0303
Phone: 225-924-1431
Website: https://cicla.org
Facebook: https://www.facebook.com/
brcrisisinterventioncenter

MAINE

Crisis and Counseling Centers
Address: 10 Caldwell Rd., August, ME 04330
Hotline: 888-568-1112
Phone: 207-626-3448
Fax: 207-621-6228
Website: http://www.crisisandcounseling.org

MARYLAND

Baltimore Crisis Response
Address: 2041 East Fayette St., Baltimore, MD 21231
Hotline: 410-433-5175
Hotline TDD: 410-433-7050
Phone: 410-433-5255
Fax: 410-433-6795
Website: http://www.bcresponse.org

Frederick County Hotline
Address: 226 South Jefferson St., Frederick, MD 21701
Hotline: 301-662-2255
Phone: 301-663-0011
Fax: 301-695-4747
Website: http://www.fcmha.org

MASSACHUSETTS

The Samaritans of Boston
Address: 41 West St., 4th Floor, Boston, MA 02111
Hotline 1: 877-870-4673
Hotline 2 (Teens): 800-252-8336
Hotline 3: 617-247-0220
Hotline 4: 508-875-4500
Website: https://samaritanshope.org

MICHIGAN

Michigan Association for Suicide Prevention
Address: c/o Mary Baukus, 2220 Mershon St., Saginaw, MI
    48602
Hotline: 800-273-8255
Website: http://www.masponweb.org
Facebook: https://www.facebook.com/Michigan-
    Association-for-Suicide-Prevention-143113595749940

MINNESOTA

Canvas Health Crisis Connection
Hotline: 612-379-6363
Website: http://www.canvashealth.org/crisis-support/
    crisis-connection

MISSISSIPPI

CONTACT Helpline
Address: P.O. Box 1304, Columbus, MS 39703
Hotline: 800-377-1643
Phone: 662-327-2968
Fax: 662-244-3454
Website: http://www.contacthelplinegtrms.org
Facebook: https://www.facebook.com/Contacthelplinegtrms
Twitter: @contactgtr

MISSOURI

Life Crisis Services
Address: 2650 Olive St., St. Louis, MO 63103
Hotline 1: 314-647-4357
Hotline 2: 800-273-8255
Phone: 314-533-8200
Website: http://www.providentstl.org

MONTANA

The Help Center
Address: 421 E. Peach St., Bozeman, MT 59715
Hotline: 406-586-3333
Website: http://www.bozemanhelpcenter.org

NEBRASKA

Boys Town National Hotline
Address: 14100 Crawford St., Boys Town, NE 68010
Hotline: 800-448-3000
Phone: 402-498-1300
Website: http://www.boystown.org
Facebook: https://www.facebook.com/BoysTownMission
Twitter: @BoysTown

NEVADA

Crisis Call Center
Address: P.O. Box 8016, Reno, NV 89507
Hotline: 775-784-8090
Phone: 775-784-8085
Fax: 775-784-8083
Website: http://www.crisiscallcenter.org

NEW HAMPSHIRE

Headrest
Address: 14 Church St., Lebanon, NH 03766
Hotline: 603-448-4400
Phone: 603-448-4872
Fax: 603-448-1829
Website: http://www.headrest.org

NEW JERSEY

CONTACT of Burlington County
Address: P.O. Box 333, Moorestown, NJ 08057
Hotline 1: 856-234-8888
Hotline 2: 866-234-5006
Phone: 856-234-5484
Website: http://www.contactburlco.org

NEW MEXICO

Agora Crisis Center
Address: UNM 1; MSC 02 1675, Albuquerque, NM 87131
Hotline: 866-HELP-1-NM
Phone: 505-277-3013
Website: http://www.unm.edu/~agora

NEW YORK

Covenant House
Address: 461 Eighth Avenue, New York, NY 10001
Hotline: 800-999-9999
Phone: 800-388-3888
Website: http://www.covenanthouse.org
Facebook: https://www.facebook.com/CovenantHouse
Twitter: @CovenantHouse
YouTube: https://www.youtube.com/user/CovenantHouse

Long Island Crisis Center
Address: 2740 Martin Avenue, Bellmore, NY 11710
Hotline: 516-679-1111
Phone: 516-826-0244
Website: http://www.longislandcrisiscenter.org
Facebook: https://www.facebook.com/longisland.crisiscenter
Twitter: @LICrisisCenter

NORTH CAROLINA

REAL Crisis Intervention
Address: 1011 Anderson St., Greenville, NC 27858
Hotline: 252-758-4357
Website: http://realcrisis.org
Facebook: https://www.facebook.com/realcrisis

NORTH DAKOTA

FirstLink Hotline
Address: 4357 13th Ave. S, Ste. 107L, Fargo, ND 58103
Hotline 1: 2-1-1
Hotline 2: 701-235-7335
Phone 1: 701-293-6462
Phone 2: 888-293-6462
Fax: 701-235-2476
Website: http://myfirstlink.org/serivces/2-1-1-helpline
Facebook: https://www.facebook.com/myfirstlink
Twitter: @myfirstlink_org
YouTube: https://www.youtube.com/user/myfirstlink

OHIO

Talbert House
Address: 2600 Victory Parkway, Cincinnati, OH
45206-1711
Hotline: 513-281-2273
Phone: 513-751-7747
Fax: 513-751-8107
Website: http://www.talberthouse.org

North Central Mental Health Services
Address: 1301 North High St., Columbus, OH 43201
Hotline: 614-221-5445
Phone: 614-299-6600
Website: http://www.ncmhs.org

OKLAHOMA

Heartline
Address: Central Office, 650 S. Peoria Ave., Tulsa, OK
  74120
Hotline: 918-744-4800
Phone: 918-587-9471
Website: http://www.fcsok.org
Facebook: https://www.facebook.com/fcsok
Twitter: @FCSTulsa
YouTube: https://www.youtube.com/user/
  FamilyandChildrensOK

OREGON

Oregon Partnership-Lines for Life
Address: 5100 SW Macadam Ave., Ste. 400, Portland, OR
  97239
Hotline: 800-273-8255
Phone 1: 503-244-5211
Phone 2: 800-282-7035
Fax: 503-244-5506
Website: http://www.linesforlife.org

PENNSYLVANIA

Re:Solve Crisis Network
Address: 333 North Braddock Ave., Pittsburgh, PA 15208
Hotline: 888-796-8226
Website: http://upmc.com/Services/behavioral-health/
  Pages/resolve-crisis-network.aspx

Facebook: https://www.facebook.com/upmc
YouTube: https://www.youtube.com/upmc

RHODE ISLAND

The Samaritans of Rhode Island
Address: P.O. Box 9086, Providence, RI 02940
Hotline 1: 401-272-4044
Hotline 2: 800-365-4044
Phone: 401-721-5220
Website: http://www.samaritansri.org

SOUTH CAROLINA

Mental Health America of South Carolina
Address: 1823 Gadsden St., Columbia, SC 29201
Hotline: 800-273-8255
Phone: 803-779-5363
Fax: 864-467-3547
Website: http://www.mha-sc.org

SOUTH DAKOTA

HELP!Line Center
Address: 1000 N. West Ave., Ste. 310, Sioux Falls, SD
57104
Hotline 1: 2-1-1
Hotline 2: 605-334-6646
Website: http://www.helplinecenter.org
Facebook: https://www.facebook.com/HelplineCenter
Twitter: @HelplineCenter

TENNESSEE

The Crisis Center of Family & Children's Service
Address: 1704 Heiman St., Nashville, TN 37208
Hotline: 615-244-7444
Phone: 615-320-0591
Website: http://www.fcsnashville.org

TEXAS

Texas Department of State Health Services
Address: 1100 West 49th St., Austin, TX 78756
Hotline: 800-273-8255
Phone: 512-776-7111
Website: https://www.dshs.texas.gov/mhsa/suicide/Suicide-Prevention.aspx

Texas Suicide Prevention
Hotline: 800-273-8255
Website: http://www.texassuicideprevention.org

UTAH

UNI CrisisLine
Address: University Neuropsychiatric Institute, 501 Chipeta Way, Salt Lake City, UT 84108
Hotline: 801-587-3000
Phone: 801-587-1055
Website: http://healthcare.utah.edu/uni/crisisline

VERMONT

Vermont 2-1-1
Address: P.O. Box 111, Essex Junction, VT 05453
Hotline 1: 2-1-1
Hotline 2: 866-652-4636
Fax: 802-861-2544
Website: http://www.vermont211.org

Facebook: https://www.facebook.com/Vermont211
YouTube: https://www.youtube.com/211vermont

VIRGINIA

CrisisLink
Address: 1761 Old Meadow Road, Ste. 100, McLean, VA
22102
Hotline: 703-527-4077
Hotline TDD: 7-1-1
Phone: 703-536-9000
Website: http://www.crisislink.org
Facebook: https://www.facebook.com/crisislink

WASHINGTON

Crisis Clinic
Address: 9725 3rd Avenue NE, Ste. 300, Seattle, WA 98115
Hotline: 866-427-4747
Phone: 206-461-3210
Fax: 206-461-8368
Website: http://www.crisisclinic.org
Facebook: https://www.facebook.com/
CrisisClinicKingCounty
Twitter: @CrisisClinic

WEST VIRGINIA

Valley HealthCare System
Address: 301 Scott Avenue, Morgantown, WV 26508
Hotline: 800-232-0020
Phone: 304-296-1731
Fax: 304-225-2288
Website: http://www.valleyhealthcare.org

WISCONSIN

Crisis Center of Family Services

Address: Family Services of Northeast Wisconsin, Inc., 300
    Crooks St., Green Bay, WI 54305
Hotline: 920-436-8888
Phone: 920-436-6800
Fax: 920-432-5966
Website: http://www.familyservicesnew.org
Facebook: https://www.facebook.com/familyservicesnew

WYOMING

Wyoming Behavioral Institute

Address: 2521 E. 15th St., Casper, WY 82609
Hotline: 800-457-9312
Phone: 307-237-7444
Fax: 307-472-2297
Website: http://www.wbihelp.com

CANADIAN RESOURCES

ALBERTA

Doctor Margaret Savage Crisis Centre
Address: Box 419, Cold Lake, AB T9M 1P1
Hotline: 866-594-0533
Phone: 780-594-5095
Fax: 780-594-7304
Website: http://www.dmscc.ca

BRITISH COLUMBIA

The Crisis Intervention and Suicide Prevention Centre of British Columbia
Address: 763 East Broadway, Vancouver, BC V5T 1X8
Hotline: 800-784-2433
Phone: 604-872-1811
Fax: 604-879-6216
Website: http://www.crisiscentre.bc.ca

MANITOBA

The Manitoba Suicide Line
Address: c/o Klinic Community Health, 870 Portage Ave., Winnipeg, MB, R3G 0P1
Hotline: 877-435-7170
Phone: 204-571-4182
Fax: 204-571-4184
Website: http://www.reasontolive.ca
Facebook: https://www.facebook.com/pages/Reason-To-Live-Manitoba-Suicide-Line/149395961783773

New Brunswick

New Brunswick Suicide Prevention Resource Center
Address: 403 Regent St. Ste. 202, Fredericton, NB E3B 3X6
Hotline: 800-667-5005
Phone: 506-455-5231
Fax: 506-459-3878
Website: http://nb.cmha.ca

Newfoundland and Labrador

Mental Health Crisis Centre
Address: 47 St. Clare Ave., St. John's, NF A1C 2J9
Hotline: 888-737-4668
Phone: 709-737-4271
Website: https://suicideprevention.ca/
    newfoundland-labrador-crisis-centres

Nova Scotia

Mental Health Mobile Crisis Team
Hotline: 902-429-8167
Website: http://www.nshealth.ca/service-details/Mental%20
    Health%20Mobile%20Crisis%20Telephone%20Line

Ontario

Distress Center Ontario
Website: http://www.dcontario.org/centres.html
See site for local crisis centers and hotlines.

Prince Edward Island

Island Helpline
Address: P.O. Box 1033, Fredericton, PE E3B 5C2
Hotline: 800-218-2885
Website: https://suicideprevention.ca/
    prince-edward-island-crisis-centres

QUÉBEC

Centre de Prévention du Suicide de Québec
Address: 8180 Boulevard Pierre-Bertrand Nord, Québec,
G2K 1W1
Hotline: 866-277-3553
Phone: 418-683-4588
Fax: 418-683-5956
Website: http://www.cpsquebec.ca

SASKATCHEWAN

Website: https://suicideprevention.ca/
saskatchewan-crisis-centres
See site for local crisis centers and hotlines.

Additional Suggested Readings

King, K. A., Vidourek, R. A., & Strader, J. L. (2008). University students' perceived self-efficacy in identifying suicidal warning signs and helping suicidal friends find campus intervention resources. *Suicide and Life-Threatening Behavior, 38,* 608–617.

Nadeem, E., Santiago, C. D., Kataoka, S. H., Chang, V. Y., & Stein, B. D. (2016). School personnel experiences in notifying parents about their child's risk for suicide: Lessons learned. *The Journal of School Health, 86,* 3–10. https://doi.org/10.1111/josh.12346

Nadeem, E., Kataoka, S. H., Chang, V. Y., Vona, P., Wong, M., & Stein, B. D. (2011). The role of teachers in school-based suicide prevention: A qualitative study of school staff perspectives. *School Mental Health, 3,* 209–221. https://doi.org/10.1007/s12310-011-9056-7

Petrova, M., Wyman, P. A., Schmeelk-Cone, K., & Pisani, A. R. (2015). Positive-themed suicide prevention messages delivered by adolescent peer leaders: Proximal impact on classmates' coping attitudes and perceptions of adult support. *Suicide and Life-Threatening Behavior, 45,* 651–663. https://doi.org/10.1111/sltb.12156

Strunk, C. M., Sorter, M. T., Ossege, J., & King, K. A. (2014). Emotionally troubled teens' help-seeking behaviors: An evaluation of Surviving the Teens® suicide prevention and depression awareness program. *The Journal of School Nursing, 30,* 366–375. https://doi.org/10.1177/1059840513511494

Wyman, P. A., Brown, C. H., LoMurray, M., Schmeelk-Cone, K., Petrova, M., Yu, Q., . . . Wang, W. (2010). An outcome evaluation of the sources of strength suicide prevention program delivered by adolescent peer leaders in high schools. *American Journal of Public Health, 100,* 1653–1661. https://doi.org/10.2105/AJPH.2009.190025

REFERENCES

American Association of Suicidology. (n.d.). *Know the warning signs of suicide.* Retrieved from http://www.suicidology.org/ resources/warning-signs

American College Health Association. (2016). *American College Health Association—National college health assessment II: Undergraduate students reference group data report, Fall 2015.* Hanover, MD: Author.

Bain, S. K., Bliss, S. L., Choate, S. M., & Sager Brown, K. (2007). Serving children who are gifted: Perceptions of undergraduates planning to become teachers. *Journal for the Education of the Gifted, 30,* 450–478.

Baker, J. A. (1995). Depression and suicidal ideation among academically talented adolescents. *Gifted Child Quarterly, 39,* 218–223.

Birkett, M., Espelage, D. L., & Koenig, B. (2009). LGB and questioning students in schools: The moderating effects of homophobic bullying and school climate on negative outcomes. *Journal of Youth and Adolescence, 38,* 989–1000.

Brown, B. B., & Steinberg, L. (1990). Skirting the brain-nerd connection: Academic achievement and social acceptance. *Education Digest, 15*(4), 57–60.

Cassady, J. C., & Cross, T. L. (2006). A factorial representation of suicidal ideation among academically gifted adolescents. *Journal for the Education of the Gifted, 29,* 290–304.

Centers for Disease Control and Prevention. (2009). *Death rates for selected causes by 10-year age groups, race, and sex: Death registration states, 1900–32, and United States, 1933–98.* Retrieved from https://www.cdc.gov/nchs/nvss/mortality/hist290.htm

Centers for Disease Control and Prevention. (2013). *Trends in the prevalence of suicide–related behavior: National Youth Risk Behavior Survey: 1991–2013.* Washington, DC: Division of Adolescent and School Health, National Center for HIV/ AIDS, Viral Hepatitis, STD, and TB Prevention, Centers for Disease Control. Retrieved from https://www.cdc.gov/ healthyyouth/data/yrbs/pdf/trends/us_suicide_trend_yrbs. pdf

Centers for Disease Control and Prevention. (2015a). *Suicide facts at a glance.* Washington, DC: National Center for Injury Prevention and Control, Division of Violence Prevention.

Centers for Disease Control and Prevention. (2015b). *Years of potential life lost (YPLL) reports, 1999–2015.* Retrieved from https://webappa.cdc.gov/sasweb/ncipc/ypll10.html

Centers for Disease Control and Prevention. (2015c). *National violent death reporting system (NVDRS) coding manual revised.* Washington, DC: National Center for Injury Prevention and Control, Centers for Disease Control and Prevention. Retrieved from https://www.cdc.gov/violenceprevention/pdf/ nvdrs_web_codingmanual.pdf

Centers for Disease Control and Prevention. (2016). Youth risk behavior surveillance—United States, 2015. *Morbidity and Mortality Weekly Report, 65*(6), 1–174. Retrieved from https:// www.cdc.gov/mmwr/volumes/65/ss/ss6506a1.htm?s_cid=s s6506a1_w

Centers for Disease Control and Prevention. (2017a). *Fatal injury reports, national, regional and state, 1981–2015.* Retrieved from https://webappa.cdc.gov/sasweb/ncipc/mortrate.html

Centers for Disease Control and Prevention. (2017b). *National vital statistics reports.* Retrieved from http://www.cdc.gov/ nchs/products/nvsr.htm

Coker, T. R., Austin, S. B., & Schuster, M. A. (2010). The health and health care of lesbian, gay, and bisexual adolescents. *Annual Review of Public Health, 31*, 457–477.

Coleman, L. (1985). *Schooling the gifted.* Menlo Park, CA: Addison-Wesley.

Coleman, L. (2011). Lived experience, mixed messages, and stigma. In T. L. Cross & J. R. Cross (Eds.), *Handbook for counselors serving students with gifts and talents* (pp. 371–392). Waco, TX: Prufrock Press.

Coleman, L. J., & Cross, T. L. (1988). Is being gifted a social handicap? *Journal for the Education of the Gifted, 11,* 41–56.

Coleman, L. J., & Cross, T. L. (2000). Social-emotional development and the personal experience of giftedness. In K. A. Heller, F. J. Mönks, R. J. Sternberg, & R. F. Subotnik (Eds.), *International handbook of giftedness and talent* (pp. 203–212). Oxford, England: Elsevier.

Coleman, L. J., & Guo, A. (2013). Exploring children's passion for learning in six domains. *Journal for the Education of the Gifted, 36,* 155–175.

Coleman, L. J., Micko, K. J., & Cross, T. L. (2015). Twenty-five years of research on the lived experiences of being gifted in school: Capturing the students' voices. *Journal for the Education of the Gifted, 38,* 358–376.

Crosby, A. E., Ortega, L., & Melanson, C. (2011). *Self-directed violence surveillance: Uniform definitions and recommended data elements.* Atlanta, GA: Centers for Disease Control and Prevention.

Cross, J. R. (2015). Peer relationships of gifted children. In M. Neihart, S. Pfeiffer, & T. L. Cross (Eds.), *The social and emotional development of gifted children: What do we know?* (2nd ed., pp. 41–54). Waco, TX: Prufrock Press.

Cross, J. R., & Cross, T. L. (2015a). Clinical and mental health issues in counseling the gifted individual. *Journal of Counseling & Development, 93,* 163–172.

Cross, J. R., & Cross, T. L. (2015b). Addressing concerns about the social and emotional needs of gifted students. In J. H. Robins (Ed.), *Gifted Education in Ireland and the United States* (pp. 177–203). Dublin, Ireland: CTYI Press.

Cross, J. R., Cross, T. L., & Frazier, A. D. (2013). Student and teacher attitudes toward giftedness in a two laboratory school environment: A case for conducting a needs assessment.

NALS Journal, 5(1). Retrieved from http://digitalcommons. ric.edu/nals/vol5/iss1/1

Cross, T. L. (1996a). Examining claims about gifted children and suicide. *Gifted Child Today, 19*(1), 46–48.

Cross, T. L. (1996b). Social and emotional needs of gifted students: Psychological autopsy provides insight into gifted adolescent suicide. *Gifted Child Today, 19*(3), 22–50.

Cross, T. L. (2008). Suicide. In J. A. Plucker & C. M. Callahan (Eds.), *Critical issues and practices in gifted education: What the research says* (pp. 629–639). Waco, TX: Prufrock Press.

Cross, T. L. (2017). *On the social and emotional lives of gifted children* (5th ed.). Waco, TX: Prufrock Press.

Cross, T. L., Andersen, L., & Mammadov, S. (2015). Effects of academic acceleration on the social and emotional lives of gifted students. In S. G. Assouline, N. Colangelo, J. VanTassel-Baska, & A. Lupkowski-Shoplik (Eds.), *A nation empowered: Evidence trumps the excuses holding back America's brightest students* (Vol. 2, pp. 31–42). Iowa City: University of Iowa, The Connie Belin & Jacqueline N. Blank International Center for Gifted Education and Talent Development.

Cross, T. L., Cassady, J. C., & Miller, T. (2006). Suicidal ideation and psychological type in gifted adolescents. *Gifted Child Quarterly, 19*, 46–48.

Cross, T. L., Coleman, L. J., & Stewart, R. A. (1993). The school-based social cognition of gifted adolescents: An exploration of the stigma of giftedness paradigm. *Roeper Review, 16*, 37–40.

Cross, T. L., Coleman, L. J., & Terhaar-Yonkers, M. (1991). The social cognition of gifted adolescents in schools: Managing the stigma of giftedness. *Journal for the Education of the Gifted, 15*, 44–55.

Cross, T. L., Cook, R. S., & Dixon, D. N. (1996). Psychological autopsies of three academically talented adolescents who committed suicide. *Journal of Secondary Gifted Education, 7*, 403–409.

Cross, T. L., & Cross, J. R. (2017a). Maximizing potential: A school-based conception of psychosocial development. *High*

Ability Studies, 28, 43–58. doi:10.1080/13598139.2017.1292 896

Cross, T. L., & Cross, J. R. (2017b). Suicide among students with gifts and talents. In S. Pfeiffer, E. Shaunessy-Dedrick, & M. Foley-Nicpon (Eds.), *APA handbook of giftedness and talent* (pp. 601–614). Washington, DC: American Psychological Association.

Cross, T. L., Cross, J. R., & Andersen, L. (2017). The school-based psychosocial curriculum model. In J. VanTassel-Baska & C. A. Little (Eds.), *Content-based curriculum for high-ability learners* (3rd ed., pp. 383–407). Waco, TX: Prufrock Press.

Cross, T. L., Cross, J. R., Mammadov, S., Ward, T. J., Speirs Neumeister, K. L., & Andersen, L. (2017). Psychological heterogeneity among honors college students. *Manuscript in review.*

Cross, T. L., Gust-Brey, K., & Ball, B. (2002). A psychological autopsy of the suicide of an academically gifted student: Researchers' and parents' perspectives. *Gifted Child Quarterly, 46,* 247–264.

Cross, T. L., Stewart, R. A., & Coleman, L. J. (2003). Phenomenology and its implications for gifted studies research: Investigating the *Lebenswelt* of academically gifted students attending an elementary magnet school. *Journal for the Education of the Gifted, 26,* 201–220.

Cross, T. L., & Swiatek, M. A. (2009). Social coping among academically gifted students in a residential setting: A longitudinal study. *Gifted Child Quarterly, 53,* 25–33.

Dabrowski, K. (1964). *Positive disintegration.* Boston, MA: Little, Brown.

Dabrowski, K. (1972). *Psychoneurosis is not an illness.* London, England: Gryf.

Delisle, J. (1986). Death with honors: Suicide among gifted adolescents. *Journal of Counseling and Development, 64,* 558–560.

Delisle, J. R. (1990). The gifted adolescent at risk: Strategies and resources for suicide prevention among gifted youth. *Journal of Education of the Gifted, 13,* 212–228.

DeLisle, M. M., & Holden, R. R. (2009). Differentiating between depression, hopelessness, and psychache in university undergraduates. *Measurement and Evaluation in Counseling and Development, 42,* 46–63.

Dixon, D. N., Cross, T. L., Cook, R., & Scheckel, J. (1995). Gifted-adolescent suicide: Database vs. speculation. *Research Briefs, 10*(1), 45–50.

Durkheim, E. (1951). *Suicide.* Glencoe, IL: The Free Press.

Eckert, T. L., Miller, D. N., DuPaul, G. J., & Riley-Tillman, T. C. (2003). Adolescent suicide prevention: School psychologists' acceptability of school-based programs. *School Psychology Review, 32,* 57–76.

Erikson, E. H. (1950/1980). Growth and crises of the healthy personality. In E. H. Erikson (Ed.), *Identity and the life cycle* (pp. 51–107). New York, NY: Norton.

Erikson, E. H. (1963). *Childhood and society* (2nd ed.). New York, NY: Norton.

Every Student Succeeds Act of 2015, Pub. L. No. 114-95 § 114 Stat. 1177 (2015–2016).

Falk, G. (2001). *Stigma: How we treat outsiders.* Amherst, NY: Prometheus Books.

Fleith, D. S. (1998). Suicide among talented youngsters: A sociocultural perspective. *Gifted Education International, 13,* 113–120.

Fleith, D. D. (2001, Spring). Suicide among gifted adolescents: How to prevent it. *National Research Center for the Gifted and Talented Newsletter.* Retrieved from http://www.nrcgt.uconn.edu/newsletters/spring012

Foucault, M. (1978). *The history of sexuality. Volume 1: An introduction.* (R. Hurley, Trans.). New York, NY: Pantheon. (Original work published 1976)

Goffman, E. (1963). *Stigma: Notes on the management of spoiled identity.* New York, NY: The Free Press.

Gould, M. S., & Shaffer, D. (1986). The impact of suicide in television movies. *New England Journal of Medicine, 315,* 690–694.

Gould, M. A., Greenberg, T., Velting, D. M., & Shaffer, D. (2003). Youth suicide risk and preventive interventions: A review of the past 10 years. *Journal of the American Academy of Child and Adolescent Psychiatry, 42,* 386–405.

Gross, M. U. M. (2003). *Exceptionally gifted children* (2nd ed.). New York, NY: Routledge.

Grossman, A. H., & D'Augelli, A. R. (2007). Transgender youth and life-threatening behaviors. *Suicide and Life-Threatening Behavior, 37,* 527–537.

Heilbron, N., Compton, J. S., Daniel, S. S., & Goldston, D. B. (2010). The problematic label of suicide gesture: Alternatives for clinical research and practice. *Professional Psychology: Research and Practice, 41,* 221–227. http://dx.doi.org/10.1037/a0018712

Hewitt, P. L., & Flett, G. L. (1991). Perfectionism in the self and social contexts: Conceptualization, assessment, and association with psychopathology. *Journal of Personality and Social Psychology, 60,* 456–470.

Hewitt, P. L., & Flett, G. L. (2004). *Multidimensional Perfectionism Scale: Technical manual.* North Tonawanda, NY: Multi-Health Systems.

Hewitt, P. L., Flett, G. L., Sherry, S. B., & Caelian, C. (2006). Trait perfectionism dimensions and suicidal behavior. In T. E. Ellis (Ed.), *Cognition and suicide: Theory, research, and therapy* (pp. 215–235). Washington, DC: American Psychological Association.

Howley, C., Howley, A., & Pendarvis, E. (1995). *Out of our minds: Anti-intellectualism and talent development for American schooling.* New York, NY: Teachers College Press.

Howley, C., Howley, A., & Pendarvis, E. (2017). *Out of our minds: Turning the tide of anti-intellectualism in American schools* (2nd ed.). Waco, TX: Prufrock Press.

Husserl, E. (1970). *The crisis of European sciences and transcendental phenomenology: An introduction to phenomenology* (D. Carr, Trans.). Evanston, IL: Northwestern University Press.

Hyatt, L. (2010). A case study of the suicide of a gifted female adolescent: Implications for prediction and prevention. *Journal for the Education of the Gifted, 33,* 514–535.

Jack, B. (2014). Goethe's *Werther* and its effects. *The Lancet Psychiatry, 1,* 18–19.

Jobes, D. A., Berman, A. L., O'Carroll, P. W., Eastgard, S., & Knickmeyer, S. (1996). The Kurt Cobain suicide crisis: Perspectives from research, public health, and the news media. *Suicide and Life-Threatening Behavior, 26,* 260–271.

John, A., Hawton, K., Gunnell, D., Lloyd, K., Scourfield, J., Jones, P. A. . . . & Dennis, M. S. (2017). Newspaper reporting on a cluster of suicides in the UK: A study of article characteristics using PRINTQUAL. *Crisis, 38,* 17–25.

Johnson, J., Panagioti, M., Bass, J., Ramsey, L., & Harrison, R. (2017). Resilience to emotional distress in response to failure, error or mistakes: A systematic review. *Clinical Psychology Review, 52,* 19–42.

Johnson, M. C. (1994). Cerulean sky: A gifted student explains his differences and difficulties. *Gifted Child Today, 17*(5), 20–21, 42.

Kaiser, C. F., & Berndt, D. J. (1985). Predictors of loneliness in the gifted adolescent. *Gifted Child Quarterly, 29,* 74–77.

Kalesan, B., Villarreal, M. D., Keyes, K. M., & Galea, S. (2016). Gun ownership and social gun culture. *Injury Prevention, 22,* 216–220.

Kanevsky, L., & Keighley, T. (2003). To produce or not to produce? Understanding boredom and the honor in underachievement. *Roeper Review, 26,* 20–28.

Katz, C., Bolton, S.-L., Katz, L. Y., Isaak, C., Tilston-Jones, T., Sareen, J., & Swampy Cree Suicide Prevention Team. (2013). A systematic review of school-based suicide prevention programs. *Depression and Anxiety, 30,* 1030–1045.

King, C. (1997). Suicidal behavior in adolescence. In R. Maris, M. Silverman, & S. Canetto (Eds.), *Review of suicidology* (pp. 61–95). New York, NY: Guilford.

Knapp, J. D. (2017). "13 Reasons Why": Canadian schools ban all talk, issue warnings about Netflix series. *Variety.* Retrieved from http://variety.com/2017/tv/news/13-reasons-why-netflix-canadian-school-bans-talk-1202403323

Kochanek, K. D., Murphy, S. L., Xu, J., & Tejada-Vera, B. (2016). Deaths: Final data for 2014. *National Vital Statistics Reports, 65*(4). Washington, DC: U.S. Department of Health and Human Services.

Lester, D. (2011). Extraversion and suicidal behavior. In A. M. Columbus (Ed.), *Advances in psychology research* (Vol. 78, pp. 113–121). Hauppauge, NY: Nova Science.

Ludwig, A. (1995). *The price of greatness.* New York, NY: Guilford.

Mead, M. (1954). The gifted child in the American culture of today. *The Journal of Teacher Education, 5,* 211–214.

Metha, A., & McWhirter, E. H. (1997). Suicide ideation, depression, and stressful life events among gifted adolescents. *Journal for the Education of the Gifted, 20,* 284–304.

Miller, M., Azrael, D., & Barber, C. (2012). Suicide mortality in the United States: The importance of attending to method in understanding population-level disparities in the burden of suicide. *Annual Review of Public Health, 33,* 393–408.

Niederkrotenthaler, T., Fu, K., Yip, P. S. F., Fong, D. Y. T., Stack, S., Cheng, Q., & Pirkis, J. (2012). Changes in suicide rates following media reports on celebrity suicide: A meta-analysis. *Journal of Epidemiology and Community Health, 66,* 1037–1042.

No Child Left Behind Act, 20 U.S.C. §6301 (2001).

Peine, M., & Coleman, L. J. (2010). The phenomenon of waiting in class. *Journal for the Education of the Gifted, 24,* 220–244.

Pelkonen, M., & Marttunen, M. (2003). Child and adolescent suicide: Epidemiology, risk factors, and approaches to prevention. *Pediatric Drugs, 5,* 243–265.

Peterson, J. S. (1993). What we learned from Genna. *Gifted Child Today, 16,* 15–16.

Peterson, J. S. (2014). Giftedness, trauma, and development: A qualitative, longitudinal case study. *Journal for the Education of the Gifted, 37,* 295–318.

Peterson, J., & Ray, K. (2006). Bullying among the gifted: The subjective experience. *Gifted Child Quarterly, 50,* 252–269.

Phillips, D. P. (1974). The influence of suggestion on suicide: Substantive and theoretical implications of the Werther effect. *American Sociological Review, 39,* 340–354.

Reynolds, C. R. (1987). Raising intelligence: Clever Hans, Candides, and the miracle in Milwaukee. *Journal of School Psychology, 25,* 309–312.

Roy, E. A. (2017). 13 Reasons Why: New Zealand bans under-18s from watching suicide drama without adult. *The Guardian.* Retrieved from https://www.theguardian.com/world/2017/apr/28/13-reasons-why-new-zealand-bans-under-18s-from-watching-suicide-drama-without-adult

Rudd, M. D., Berman, A. L., Joiner, T. E., Nock, M. K., Silverman, M. M., Mandrusiak, M., & White, T. (2006). Warning signs for suicide: Theory, research, and clinical applications. *Suicide and Life-Threatening Behavior, 36,* 255–262. doi:10.1521/suli.2006.36.3.255

Russell, S. T., & Joyner, K. (2001). Adolescent sexual orientation and suicide risk: Evidence from a national study. *American Journal of Public Health, 91,* 1276–1281.

Ryan, C., Huebner, D., Diaz, R. M., & Sanchez, J. (2009). Family rejection as a predictor of negative health outcomes in white and Latino lesbian, gay, and bisexual young adults. *Pediatrics, 123,* 346–352.

Sak, U. (2004). A synthesis of research on psychological types of gifted adolescents. *Journal of Secondary Gifted Education, 15,* 70–79.

Scheiber, N. (2013, March 11). So open it hurts: What the Internet did to Aaron Swartz. *The New Republic,* 16–23.

Sedillo, P. J. (2015). Gay gifted adolescent suicide and suicidal ideation literature: Research barriers and limitations. *Gifted Child Today, 38,* 114–120.

Seiden, R. H. (1966). Campus tragedy: A study of student suicide. *Journal of Abnormal Psychology, 71,* 389–399.

Shneidman, E. (1981). Suicide thoughts and reflections. *Suicide and Life-Threatening Behavior, 11,* 198–231.

Shneidman, E. S. (1993). *Suicide as psychache: A clinical approach to self-destructive behavior.* Northvale, NJ: Jason Aronson.

Shneidman, E. S. (1998). *The suicidal mind.* Oxford, England: Oxford University Press.

Siegle, D., Wilson, H. E., & Little, C. A. (2013). A sample of gifted and talented educators' attitudes about academic acceleration. *Journal of Advanced Academics, 24,* 27–51. doi:10.1177/1932202X12472491

Southern, W. T., & Jones, E. D. (Eds.). (1991). *The academic acceleration of gifted children.* New York, NY: Teachers College Press.

Speirs Neumeister, K. (2015). Perfectionism in gifted children. In M. Neihart, S. I. Pfeiffer, & T. L. Cross (Eds.), *The social and emotional development of gifted children: What do we know?* (2nd ed., pp. 29–40). Waco, TX: Prufrock Press.

Stillion, J. M., & McDowell, E. E. (1996). *Suicide across the life span.* Washington, DC: Taylor & Francis.

Stillion, J. M., McDowell, E., & May, J. (1984). Developmental trends and sex differences in adolescent attitudes toward suicide. *Death Education, 8,* 81–90.

Stoeber, J., & Otto, K. (2006). Positive conceptions of perfectionism: Approaches, evidence, challenges. *Personality and Social Psychology Review, 10,* 295–319. doi:10.1207/s15327 957pspr1004 2

Street, S., & Kromney, J. D. (1994). Relationship between suicidal behavior and personality types. *Suicide and Life-Threatening Behavior, 24,* 282–292.

Subotnik, R. F., Olszewski-Kubilius, P., & Worrell, F. C. (2011). Rethinking giftedness and gifted education: A proposed direction forward based on psychological science. *Psychological Science in the Public Interest, 12,* 3–54.

Tannenbaum, A. J. (1962). *Adolescent attitude toward academic brilliance.* New York, NY: Bureau of Publications, Teachers College, Columbia University.

Tannenbaum, A. (1983). *Gifted children.* New York, NY: Macmillan.

Turner, J. C., Leno, E. V., & Keller, A. (2013). Causes of mortality among American college students: A pilot study. *Journal of College Student Psychotherapy, 27,* 31–42.

U.S. Census Bureau. (n.d.). *Census regions and divisions of the United States.* Retrieved from https://www2.census.gov/geo/pdfs/maps-data/maps/reference/us_regdiv.pdf

White, J. (2016). *Preventing youth suicide: A guide for practitioners.* Victoria, British Columbia: Ministry of Children and Family Development. Retrieved from http://www2.gov.bc.ca/assets/gov/health/managing-your-health/mental-health-substance-use/child-teen-mental-health/preventing_youth_suicide_practitioners_guide.pdf

Wilcox, H. C., Kellam, S. G., Brown, C. H., Poduska, J., Ialongo, N. S., Wang, W., & Anthony, J. C. (2008). The impact of two universal randomized first- and second-grade classroom interventions on young adult suicide ideation and attempt. *Drug and Alcohol Dependence, 95* (Suppl 1), S60–S73.

World Health Organization. (2008). *Preventing suicide: A resource for media professionals.* Geneva, Switzerland: Author. Retrieved from http://apps.who.int/iris/bitstream/10665/43954/1/9789241597074_eng.pdf

Zabloski, J., & Milacci, F. (2012). Gifted dropouts: Phenomenological case studies of rural gifted students. *Journal of Ethnographic & Qualitative Research, 6,* 175–190.

ABOUT THE AUTHORS

Tracy L. Cross, Ph.D., holds an endowed chair as the Jody and Layton Smith Professor of Psychology and Gifted Education and is the executive director of the Center for Gifted Education and Institute for Research on the Suicide of Gifted Students at William & Mary. Previously he served Ball State University as the George and Frances Ball Distinguished Professor of Psychology and Gifted Studies, the executive director of the Center for Gifted Studies and Talent Development, and the Institute for Research on the Psychology of Gifted Students. For 9 years he served as the executive director of the Indiana Academy for Science, Mathematics, and Humanities, a residential high school for intellectually gifted adolescents. He has published more than 150 articles and book chapters and 45 columns, has made approximately 250 presentations at conferences, and has published 10 books. He has edited seven journals, including many in the field of gifted studies (*Gifted Child Quarterly, Roeper Review, Journal of Secondary Gifted Education, Research Briefs*). He is the current editor of the *Journal for the Education of the Gifted.* He received the Distinguished Service Award from The Association for the Gifted (TAG) and the National Association for Gifted Children (NAGC), the Early Leader and Early Scholar Awards from NAGC, the Distinguished Scholar Award from NAGC, and the Lifetime Achievement Award from the MENSA Education and Research Foundation. He served as a Fulbright Scholar in Dublin, Ireland, collaborating with Dr. Colm O'Reilly, Director of the Irish Centre for Talented Youth at Dublin City University. He is serving in his second stint as the President of The Association for the

Gifted of the Council for Exceptional Children, and is President Emeritus of the National Association for Gifted Children.

He lives in Williamsburg, VA, with his wife, Dr. Jennifer Riedl Cross and their French Bulldog, Stu.

Jennifer Riedl Cross, Ph.D., is the Director of Research at the William & Mary Center for Gifted Education, where she writes grants and coordinates and conducts research. She teaches educational psychology and research methods courses for the W&M School of Education. Dr. Cross holds a doctorate in educational psychology with a specialty in cognitive and social processes from Ball State University. She is the coeditor, with Tracy L. Cross, of the *Handbook for Counselors Serving Students With Gifts and Talents.* Dr. Cross is a member of the leadership team of the newly created W&M Institute for Research on the Suicide of Gifted Students. She and Dr. Tracy L. Cross coauthored a chapter on suicide for the *American Psychological Association Handbook of Giftedness and Talent* and an article on clinical and mental health issues for a special issue of the *Journal for Counseling and Development* on gifted individuals.

With a strong interest in social justice, Dr. Cross guest edited, with Dr. James Borland, a special issue of the *Roeper Review* on the topic of gifted education and social inequality. She was an invited keynote speaker at the Roeper Institute's 2016 "A Matter of Equity Symposium" about gifted education in Detroit. She is coeditor, with Drs. Tracy L. Cross and Laurence J. Coleman, of the two-volume compendium *Critical Readings on Diversity and Gifted Students.* Dr. Cross is active with Camp Launch, the Center's residential summer camp for low-income, high-ability middle school students, where she conducts research and created the Personal Development class, which emphasizes the development of psychological resources.

As a social psychologist, Dr. Cross has studied peer relationships, with a particular focus on adolescent crowds. This interest came about through her research on the development of a social dominance orientation, an individual's preference for hierarchical or egalitarian intergroup relations. Her research in the field of gifted education emphasizes its social aspects, from individuals coping with the stigma of giftedness to attitudes toward giftedness and gifted education. She is a member of the Society for Research on Adolescence and the American Psychological Association.